WHAT DOES
GOD THINK?

TRANSGENDER PEOPLE
AND THE BIBLE

Cheryl B. Evans

What Does God Think?
Transgender People and The Bible

Cheryl B. Evans

Published by Cheryl B. Evans - Ontario, Canada
www.writtenbymom.ca

Edited by Coral Coons, Authors Talk About It
Cover Design by Emma Jackson, Saffron Rose Designs

First Published in 2017

Paperback ISBN: 978-0-9951807-4-1
eBook mobi version ISBN: 978-0-9951807-5-8
eBook epub version ISBN: 978-0-9951807-6-5

Library and Archives Canada Cataloguing in Publication

This is a work of non-fiction.
Scriptures quoted throughout are from NIV Bible unless otherwise specified.
Printed in the United States of America
First Edition - Revised Oct. 2019

Cheryl B. Evans is the author of the award winning book:
I Promised Not to Tell: Raising a transgender child
Evan's has also written a unique journal series for transgender youth and their parents. Please refer to other books by this author beginning on page 151 for more information.

Dedication

I dedicate this book to the millions of people around the world that suffer with gender dysphoria because only you can understand the true nature of what it means to be a transgender person. Society is still learning about gender dysphoria and many remain just as uneducated and ignorant as I once was. With each story that is shared and each experience that we live, we expand; we accept and even appreciate the wonderful differences and diversity that God has given us. You are brave, you are beautiful, and you are a perfect, valued child of God.

Acknowledgements

First and foremost, I must thank God. Feeling the call to write this book was difficult to ignore and throughout the process I drew strength in knowing it was for a higher purpose than my own.

I would like to thank my family; specifically, my incredible husband and two amazing children. I love you with all my heart and am so thankful to have you in my life. I need not look any farther than the three of you to know how blessed I am.

I humbly thank you, my readers, who have taken a leap of faith in picking up this book and coming along on this journey with me. You are the reason I continue to write. I am thankful to those of you who wrote to me with your words of encouragement after reading my previously published memoir. Many of you are just as passionate as I am about helping the transgender community and are making waves all on your own. There is so much to be gleaned from watching others, and seeing the strides they are making in helping us all better understand transgender people.

I would like to express my gratitude to Pastor Colby Martin for penning such an appropriate and touching foreword for this book. I am grateful to you, Colby, for not only the wonderful foreword you have written, but for your further contribution to the conversation in Chapter Four. I believe your words will bless those whose ears they fall upon and encourage all of us to love more inclusively.

I would like to thank Koreen Pagano for her valuable contribution to this book. I draw such strength from witnessing the positive and supportive ways in which you influence the world through your own writing. As a parent of not one, but two transgender children, your insights and wisdom are invaluable to us all.

Coral Coons, your expertise and attention to detail are so appreciated. You edited this book with the care and attention you would give your own project. You pushed me to revise and polish the content the way only a skilled editor could. Thank you for all the time and dedication you gave to this book; it is better because you were a part of it.

The fabulous and skillful Emma Jackson, I can't thank you enough. You worked tirelessly with me for months to ensure I was happy with the cover design and I am. It turned out beautifully and I trust it will resonate with readers the way it has with me.

Finally, to the transgender individuals all around the world, I acknowledge you. You are the brave ones!

Acknowledgements

You wake up every morning and step out into the world that is so often unkind and unforgiving. Society knocks you down, but you fight to get back up and carry on. You withstand discrimination and, some days, you battle just to stay alive. You are the real heroes and you deserve better. You deserve to live your life free from hate, judgement, and condemnation, for you are a perfect, valued child of God.

Contents

Foreword

God has a Great Dilemma, and the dilemma is this: How to convince the human race that they are God's deeply beloved children?

One option (the kind of option that we in America might prefer) would be a grand gesture from above; some sort of cosmic display of power that no one could ignore. Get everyone's attention and then, "bam!" declare what is true.

However, I think Jesus was right when he told people, "An evil and unfaithful generation searches for a sign, but it won't receive any sign except Jonah's sign." Because let's be honest, we'd be wowed by such a show of power for a while, but eventually, it would wear off. And our children, or our children's children, would soon think we'd lost our minds.

No, solving God's dilemma can't be done by something big, showy, and instantaneous.

If the dilemma can be solved—if humans can one day truly come to accept that they are fully loved—it will have to be through something small, quiet, and slow. Something that permeates, that grows from the ground up. The mustard seed that can move mountains.

This must be why, in the Bible, we see this narrative of a gradual opening and expansion. A story that starts out small and just... keeps... growing.

From Abraham and Sarah comes a tribe of people tasked with showing the world the love of God. Out of that tribe comes a rabbi named Jesus who pushed people out from Judea to Samaria and the ends of the earth.

Then, the first apostles watched in awe as even the Gentiles showed evidence of the Divine in their life. Including an amazing story in Acts 8 about a eunuch from Ethiopia who hears from Philip about the thing God was up to in the world through Jesus. The thing about eunuchs was that they were the "sexual other" of the day. And what did Philip do? He baptized him, which is to say, he affirmed the eunuch's place in the Family of God.

The early church, when it was at its best, was caught up in the ever-expanding efforts from God to solve the great dilemma, slowly through humble people. Not through shows of power, but through displays of great love, sacrifice, and weakness—what Jesus called "the sign of Jonah."

The Christian church today has lost touch in many ways with God's momentum. Instead of continuing the expansion, instead of partnering with the Divine to bring about awareness of our belovedness, we have stopped the flow for particular groups of people. Not least of which are those who identify as LGBTQ.

Instead of following Philip (who was following Jesus) and affirming the sexual-other as a loved Child of God, we have put up a dam and restricted the free flow of grace. We have stepped between God and God's children and said, "you are broken, you are confused, you need fixed."

What Cheryl Evans does in this book is return to the work of partnering with the Divine in solving the Great Dilemma. And, as it usually has to happen, the call to love comes from the margins, from hearing the stories of those whom the powerful have cast to the sides.

Cheryl shows us that love, in its truest form, reveals God to us. If we ask the question, "what does God think," and our response does not lead us deeper into love, does not lead us back to the project of opening and expanding and including all people in to the family of God, then we are working against the flow of God's spirit.

The church needs LGBTQ people right now. The church needs transgender people right now.

Because through them, and through stories of their family showing them Divine love and acceptance, we can be called back to the great story. To the work of showing all people that they are fully loved children of God. Anything other than that will be forgotten, for only love remains.

Colby Martin

Along with his wife and Co-Pastor, Kate, Colby started San Diego's Progressive Christian Church "Sojourn Grace Collective" in the spring of 2014. Learn more at www.sojourngrace.com.

Colby is also the creator and author of *UnClobber: Rethinking Our Misuse of the Bible on Homosexuality.* Through the book, video lectures, and live events, Colby shares his story of how lining up his head and heart on the issue of homosexuality in the Bible led to him getting fired from his church and ultimately starting something new. *UnClobber* also explores what the Bible does (and does not) say about homosexuality. Learn more at www.unclobber.com.

WHAT DOES
GOD THINK?

TRANSGENDER PEOPLE
AND THE BIBLE

Cheryl B. Evans

Introduction

Wounded by the echoes of the words "not of God", the close-knit fabric of our family began to unravel. Our home, which was so often filled with laughter, became void of it. The closeness between my children gave way to emptiness as they distanced themselves from one another. Witnessing them pulling apart, I felt helpless. I wept silently in isolation as I desperately tried to hold onto my sanity. I clenched tightly to my belief that, one day, both of my children would be happy again. My comfort came in believing, as King Solomon once did, that this too shall pass.

Ours was an unanticipated journey — one that played out differently for each member of my family. Through my own experience, I came to realize the struggle I thought was unique to our family was also pulling at the heartstrings of other families. Religious people often have strong opinions about gender dysphoria and do not understand or believe how someone could be transgender. Gripped with the teachings of their faith, many struggle to understand. Long-held beliefs tell some that there is no such thing as a transgender person; that God created only male and female, thereby making acceptance difficult, if not impossible for them.

In my previous book, *I Promised Not to Tell: Raising a transgender child*, I wrote a single chapter entitled "What Does God Think?" Although that chapter was not initially long, it grew in length as a direct result of the struggle I was witnessing within my own family. After the book was published, many readers reached out to me and spoke about religion and how that single chapter affected them. The chapter had only begun to scratch the surface and, knowing there must be much more that can be said, I decided that it was a conversation well worth continuing. The idea of what God thinks deserves more thought and on a deeper level. With an open mind and an open heart, I set out to discover what is at the root of the vast differences in opinions about what God thinks, what the Bible says, and what individuals believe about transgender people. In the hopes of being able to learn more, I once again pose the question, "What does God think?"

The nature vs. nurture argument, which we will explore in this book, is tied directly to what individuals believe about transgender people and whether or not transgender people are a creation of God. Our own upbringing, church, societal norms, and cultural differences also play an important role in what we think and believe about transgender people.

Differences of opinions are healthy in society, but sometimes, opinions fuel actions that have the power to bring immense good or grievous harm to the lives of others. Tempers often flare as people become so passionate about their personal stance on a topic that we often don't pause long enough to consider the other perspective. The goal of this book is to change that by presenting the ideas and thoughts of not only myself, as the author, but of others in the fields of both science and religion. It is about having a discussion that does not judge people for whichever side of this argument they sit on. Instead, the idea here is to open the dialogue a little more and to calmly and intelligently put forth information from which we can all learn.

First, I would like to share a little about myself and why this topic is of personal interest to me. I was raised by Christian parents and baptized in the United Church of Canada as a baby. The United Church, which is Canada's largest Protestant denomination, believes and teaches that each person is unique and valuable and that diversity should be accepted with love. Like Jesus, who greeted everyone with loving kindness, the United Church is open to all people.

Being a church that does not discriminate, they ordained their first transgender minister, Cindy

Bourgeois, in 2010. The church's stance on gender is that God created male and female, as well as some individuals who are a wonderful mix of the two. The United Church may be considered progressive and overly liberal by some, but for me, the way they affirm each person is something to be celebrated. They appear to be a Christian church that keeps Christ in Christianity.

I confirmed my faith as a young teen and continued to attend The United Church through my teens and into my early twenties. I was involved in church activities and was an active member in our church's youth group.

At the age of twenty-three, I met and fell in love with the man I went on to marry. My husband, Jim, is a wonderful man who was brought up in the Catholic faith with a devout Catholic mother and a firmly believing Catholic father. Our wedding ceremony was performed in a non-denominational chapel so we could begin our marriage on religiously neutral ground. At the time of this writing, Jim and I have been happily married for almost twenty-five years. Together, Jim and I have two children, one of whom happens to be transgender. As parents, we instilled Christian values in our children and taught them the importance of showing love and kindness to others.

While I attended church regularly in my younger

years, it was not until I was in my forties that I set out to read the entire Bible. I had, like many others, read many parts of the Bible, but was always dancing from one book to another or one passage to another. This was the first time I had ever committed to reading it cover to cover in chronological order, just like I would read any other book. It took me seven months to complete. Having said that, I want you to know I do not regard myself as an expert, but simply a mother who was seeking a more detailed explanation of what the Bible says or doesn't say about transgender people. I will look to answer the tough questions about transgender people that I, as a layman myself, have spent time pondering.

If you stick with me through to the end of this book, you will find a bonus chapter I have included for you. This bonus chapter is the original *What Does God Think?* chapter that appeared in my memoir, I *Promised Not to Tell.* By sharing this bonus chapter with you, I hope it will offer you some of the back story that became the seed for this current writing.

This book is about looking at what scripture tells us or doesn't tell us about transgender people and what we know from a scientific and cultural perspective. I hope you will join me on this journey of discovery and that, at the end of our journey together, we can all walk away with a better understanding. This is a controversial topic, but I would like this book to offer us all an opportunity to learn and to try to understand and respect each other's right to have an independent opinion, whether or not we agree with that opinion. I hope we can honour one another despite any differences we might have and learn to live together harmoniously. After all, it is our diversity that makes this world such an interesting place to be. At our origin, we are all human beings — a fact that makes each of us far more alike than it makes us different.

God bless you and your family,

Cheryl B. Evans

CHAPTER 1

It's a Boy! It's a Girl! No, wait....

"As you do not know the path of the wind, or how the body is formed in a mother's womb, so you cannot understand the work of God, the maker of all things."
Ecclesiastes 11:5

Before we can discuss what God thinks about transgender people, we should address what exactly it means to say someone is transgender. Simply put, someone is transgender when the gender they identify as in their mind is different from what is suggested by their body. Our physicality, and yes, even biology, often dictates the sex we are assigned at birth. Yet, for a small percentage of people, this doesn't match up with how they mentally perceive their gender to be. The disconnect transgender people have between mind and body is known as gender dysphoria.

As much as expecting parents may think they know they are having a boy or a girl, it is possible to be surprised. In fact, even when you believe you know the sex of the baby you are having — perhaps, the sex was confirmed by an ultrasound — you may be wrong when it comes to gender. This is because many expecting parents overlook the fact that there is more to gender than just sex and the binary of male and female. For most parents, it works out okay that their expectations fall within this binary. However, occasionally, we discover a child is transgender. Having a transgender child forces parents to take a long, hard look at gender and, perhaps, open their minds and their hearts to the possibility that there is more to gender than they originally thought.

To complicate things even further, it could take many years before a parent even discovers their child is transgender. In the meantime, their own presumptions and expectations about gender can weigh heavily on both their parenting decisions and on the child's happiness. Jim and I did not become aware our youngest child was transgender until he was twelve years of age. In Jordan's pre-teen years, both Jim and I were ignorant to the fact transgender children even existed.

As parents, we choose our child's name based on the expectations we have about sex and gender. When we initially choose their clothes, we often force an outward gender expression towards male or female. We often encourage playtime activities that align with the gender we assume our child has. All of this is completely natural and how most people raise their children. Again, for most of us, no issues ever come from parenting a child based on our own expectations.

Preparing ourselves for the possibility that our child could be something other than what we believe they are is unimaginable. To find out, as I did, that my daughter wasn't my daughter after all was so completely foreign to me. I had no knowledge when my child was young about gender dysphoria, or that transgender children even existed. This is the case for many parents due to a lack of knowledge; without knowledge of something, we can't possibly prepare ourselves to deal with the reality of it.

Fortunately, with the passage of time and the spread of knowledge about transgender people, attitudes are beginning to change. More and more people are hearing the word "transgender" and starting to explore this topic for the first time. As more people become aware, some parents are choosing to place less gender bias on the way they raise their children. This means placing less emphasis on the types of toys or activities they introduce their children to. Even clothing is something parents may decide to keep more gender neutral until the child is old enough to voice an opinion regarding their own likes and dislikes.

Finding out their child is transgender is still a shock to many unsuspecting parents. With society so far behind in education and access to knowledge, it's no wonder some families face unexpected turmoil. There are also families who fear sharing their stories and worry about harsh reactions from family, friends, and even outsiders.

After my son, Jordan, came out to my husband and me, I began to write down all the things that were happening in our family. I detailed every step of what we went through; how each of us reacted to the news; and the days, months, and years that followed in helping our child transition from female to male. It was an incredibly emotional journey for all of us, and one I documented to help me process and deal with everything that was transpiring. It was a way to help me come to terms with my own feelings and aid me in managing the rollercoaster of emotions I was experiencing.

At the time, I never wanted my writing to be shared or to be published. Then, somewhere along the way, I realized something very important. If parents don't share their stories and don't allow themselves to be vulnerable, then how can we expect others to understand? We can't. I realized I had written a book that I wish had been available to me when Jordan first told us he was transgender, as I would have found it invaluable at the time. That was it, then — it had to be shared; it had to be published. *I Promised Not to Tell: Raising a transgender child* is the result of almost three years' worth of our own personal journey to discover the son we never knew we had.

One day, my youngest child told me that the thing he desired most in the world was to be a boy. At that time, I only saw him as my youngest daughter. That day, I had a decision to make, and it was one of the most difficult things I have ever faced. Now, I hope that by sharing our journey, it can bless all those that decide to read it so we can all understand and help make this world a more peaceful and accepting place for transgender children.

I Promised Not to Tell is a book parents can relate to, learn from, and even gain strength and hope from. It is now out in the world to help other parents and families know they are not alone. It is a transgender story that can help others along their own family's journey, perhaps making it just a little easier and a whole lot more understood. More than that, it is a book I hope will help humanize transgender people for all who read it as they bear witness to our experience. Perhaps, it will even challenge readers to think differently about how they react to transgender people.

Regardless of whether a person is religious, accepting, denying, or even open to having a transgender child, it is something expecting parents just don't anticipate. Most expecting parents likely don't think, or even understand, a child can be born within a gender spectrum. Instead, they focus on the binary, believing their child will be either a boy or a girl.

In most cases, when a child is born, they are assigned the sex of either male or female, but in a small minority of instances, babies are assigned intersex at birth. Most people understand when someone says, "it's a boy" or "it's a girl," and many don't ever have to think about anything beyond that initial announcement. However, for some, it's not quite that simple.

First, there are those individuals who are born intersex — meaning their biological or physical makeup differs from what we traditionally understand as a boy or a girl. While these situations are uncommon, they do happen in a small percentage of births. According to The World Health Organization, 1 in 2,000 births worldwide are visibly intersex. While some may think this is a small percentage, it equates to over three million people worldwide, which is not an insignificant number.

With some intersex conditions, it is not possible for the doctor to make a conclusive assignment of male or female at the time of birth because the sexual anatomy of the baby does not fit with what is typically expected for a male or female. In some cases, the parents are then asked which sex they wish to assign to the child based on how they would like to raise them, and then, a sex is recorded on the birth certificate based on that parental choice. If the choice the parents make does not align with how the child self-identifies as they get older, it can have devastating outcomes. The child can then become confused, distraught, and even suicidal after being raised in a fashion that does not line up with who they know themselves to be.

The parents can also go through their own torment as they come to terms with the outcome of their decision. In some cases, genetic testing can be performed to look at the child's chromosomes to discover if there is something unusual about them. There are even instances where a child's chromosomes are not aligned with what is typical for a female or male. We expect that a girl would have only XX chromosomes and a boy would have only XY chromosomes. While surprising to some, the fact of the matter is there are people who have more complicated chromosome make-ups.

On March 8, 2017, Time magazine published an article by California Superior Judge Noel Wise, in which he referred to the story that opened his own mind on gender. He shared the following:

> Many people share the ubiquitous notion that biological sex falls into two, mutually exclusive categories. In 2009, my perspective changed when I read an article written by a woman who learned shortly after marriage that she and her husband couldn't have biological children because she had an XY chromosomal pairing. While she looked like a woman, and she and her parents had always believed she was female, from a genetic standpoint, she was a man. The article was published the year after California passed Prop 8, a version of [The Defense of Marriage Act].

So, what happens when you can't assume gender from sex? In most cases, when a baby is born and ~~ned the sex of male, they self-identify as a boy. ~~eone is born and assigned the sex of female, ~~ify~~ as a girl. This makes sex and gender ~~ngeable terms. This is just not the ~~ are two *very* different things.

Societal gender roles usually place people on one side or the other of the male and female binary, but also open the door to those individuals who fall outside of these binaries. Such is the case of a transgender person; a transgender person, regardless of sex, may self-identify with a gender that is different from the sex they were assigned at birth. They may identify opposite to their assigned sex, as in the case of my son, Jordan, who was assigned female at birth, yet self-identifies as male. There are also transgender people that self-identify as neither male nor female, regardless of their sex assignment at birth. I realize this is all very confusing to most people and I appreciate that you may be thinking how impossible this all sounds. That is precisely why it is so important to put this information out there and help educate people that there is far more to sex and gender than most of us realize.

To best understand gender, it helps to think of it as a spectrum where male is at one end and female at the other. Most of the population falls to the outer ends of this spectrum, where male and female reside, while a small percentage of people self-identify somewhere in between. Anyone who self identifies their gender differently than the sex they were assigned at birth falls under the umbrella term, transgender. Those of us that do not have this disconnect between our assig sex and how we self-identify are cisgender people, and we make up the largest percentage of the population.

From a cisgender person's perspective, it is extremely difficult to understand the disconnect transgender people experience between their bodies and their minds. This disconnect varies among transgender persons from mild to severe, and each experience is as individual as the person themselves.

CHAPTER 2

Nature vs. Nurture

"Before I formed you in the womb I knew you,
before you were born I set you apart...."
Jeremiah 1:5

The dispute over the origin of transgender people always comes back to the nature vs. nurture argument. It is important that we examine the evidence on both sides to see what we can learn. If we are to believe God created transgender people, we would be saying we believe in the nature theory. If we believe transgender people are somehow against God — or, as some have so boldly said to our family, "not of God" — they would be inclined to believe the nurture theory, and likely feel being transgender is a choice and something that can be willfully changed.

I firmly stand on the nature side of this debate. My personal stance is based on years of living with a strong-willed transgender child who presented consistent, persistent, and insistent position he is male, even though he was assigned female at birth. It is also based on the many books and papers I have read on the subject and the professionals I have spoken with. Nevertheless, it is important that I offer you information so that you can draw your own conclusions, recognizing you may or may not be the parent of a transgender child, yourself.

First, I would like to discuss one of the most documented studies written in support of the nurture theory. The nurture theory suggests that gender identity is not biologically predetermined, but rather, something that is conditioned into a child. This was an idea presented by a psychologist who specialized in the study of sexual identity and the biology of gender named Dr. John Money. Dr. Money received his PhD from Harvard University in 1952 and was a professor at Johns Hopkins University, where he taught pediatrics and medical psychology from 1951 until his death in 2006. During his tenure at Johns Hopkins, he, along with his colleague, Claude Migeon (head of plastic surgery), established the Johns Hopkins Gender ity Clinic.

ney published approximately two thousand chapters, and reviews during his life. e sixty-five worldwide honours, , including the Magnus Hirschfeld

a
that

Medal in 2002. The Magnus Hirschfeld award is an award given in acknowledgement of established research in the areas of sexuality and gender within academic institutions. It is awarded by the German Society for Social-Science Sexuality Research for outstanding service to sexual science.

The award was named to honour Magnus Hirschfeld, who was a Jewish German physician and sexologist who lived from 1868 to 1935. Hirschfeld was an outspoken advocate for sexual minorities and founder of the Scientific Humanitarian Committee based in Berlin. A historian by the name of Dustin Goltz cited this committee for being the first advocacy group for homosexual and transgender rights.

Dr. Money was the one who coined the term "sexual orientation," which now commonly replaces the original term, "sexual preference." He also created the term "gender role," another term commonly used today.

Dr. Money first put forth his hypothesis that gender was something that could be socially conditioned in the 1950's, but it wasn't until the late sixties that an opportunity arose for a real-life case study. In this case study, he set out to study and follow the development of a child by the name of Bruce Reimer. The purpose of the study was to prove the child's gender identity could be conditioned into the child. Bruce Reimer was born in August of 1965 in Winnipeg, Canada. Bruce and his identical twin brother, Brian, were both born biological males. Each of the babies was healthy and free from any intersex conditions, meaning both their exterior and internal make-up was typical for little boys.

At two months of age, the boys went for what was expected to be a routine circumcision. However, things did not go as planned, and Bruce's procedure was an epic failure, which resulted in his external genitalia becoming severely damaged. This unfortunate mishap, which destroyed Bruce's penis, was blamed on faulty equipment.

The twins' parents, Ron and Janet Reimer, were presented with the injurious news and, at Dr. Money's encouragement; they consented to an operation that would further alter Bruce's genitalia to make him appear feminine. Ron and Janet were assured by Dr. Money that if they nurtured Bruce as if he was a biological girl and, when the time came, they administer female hormones to the child, they would be successful in raising their child as their daughter, rather than their son. The Reimers heeded Dr. Money's counsel and Bruce became Brenda. They went about raising their two children as brother and sister.

The children met with Dr. Money on numerous

occasions, allowing Money to study the two children and see how Brenda was living her life as a young girl. At the time, the two children had no knowledge that Brenda had, in fact, been born a boy, and keeping this information from the siblings was fundamental to the study. To prove gender could be conditioned through social construct, it was necessary for Brenda to believe she was a girl. Brenda's parents dressed her in typical girl clothes and provided her with toys that were designed for little girls. The Reimers only addressed Brenda with female pronouns and raised her completely immersed in the belief that she was a biological girl.

When Dr. Money published his initial paper on the family, to protect the children's privacy, their names were represented as John and Joan Doe, and the study was called the John/Joan Case. The paper suggested the experiment on gender conditioning was successful. It indicated that the child called Joan, who had been born male but was being raised female, was self-identifying as a young girl.

Early on, however, Brenda's mother noticed that, even though they were being consistent in the way they were raising their children, treating Brian as their son and Brenda as their daughter, both children seemed to present masculine tendencies. Brenda would be far more interested in playing with Brian's toys than her own. As Brenda became a little older, she wanted to play with boys, not girls. This didn't fare well for Brenda, though, because the other boys were not interested in her playing with them, and she really wasn't interested in what the other little girls were playing. This caused Brenda to feel isolated and unhappy. There was an internal struggle that Brenda did not understand, but how could she understand without the knowledge and truth about her own birth?

Years passed and, because Brenda continued to live as a girl, Dr. Money continued to publish that the John/Jane Case had been successful. He claimed the study showed a person's gender identity could be conditioned, and that Brenda was living proof it could be done.

Meanwhile, the internal torment continued for Brenda, and at the age of fourteen, she attempted suicide. Witnessing the obvious sadness in Brenda, the Reimers decided it was time to tell their children the truth. Brenda immediately expressed how everything she was feeling now made sense, and within a short time, decided to revert to being a boy. Brenda became David, and had surgery to re-construct his male sex organs. He went on to marry a woman with three children, making him a stepfather.

Unfortunately, due to extenuating circumstances, David took his own life at the age of thirty-nine. Years before doing so, he came forward, publicly announcing himself as being Joan in Dr. Money's John/Joan Case. He spoke about the internal suffering he had been through and negated all the positive study claims Dr. Money had been proclaiming. David proved that, at least in his case, nature had won out over nurture when it came to his gender identity.

The results live on to help others who have found themselves in similar situations and serve to caution doctors on the harm that can be caused by performing any kind of sex assignment surgery on intersex children. When doctors and parents make decisions about a baby's gender, and parents proceed to raise children based on these decisions, they could be setting their children up for years of unnecessary suffering. Would it not be more prudent to let intersex children be raised in a gender-neutral environment, for at least as long as it takes for them to articulate what it is they want for themselves?

Now, I understand after reviewing the David Reimer story that, even if we accept that nature won out, it is not answering the question of how this relates to transgender people. David was born a biological male and the fact that he self-identified as male only tells us he is a cisgender person. A cisgender person, as previously discussed, is someone who self-identifies with the biological sex they were assigned at birth.

You may be wondering why I just don't say the majority of the population is *normal*, rather than cisgender. Well, to say *normal* would be offensive to anyone who does not have a gender identity that aligns with their birth sex, and suggest they are not normal. This would be unkind, so what I will say is that it is typical that a person self-identifies with a gender that aligns with their birth sex.

The real question is: can we say a transgender person has a cause for their gender dysphoria that is based in nature? Can we conclude that the disconnect between their mind and their body, which we call gender dysphoria, is the result of a biological condition? Do we say that if someone is transgender, that was already a part of them before they were born? Or do we conclude that society or social conditioning somehow causes the gender dysphoria experienced by a transgender person?

First, I believe we can still use the David Reimer case to say that people cannot be conditioned to adopt a gender identity that isn't inherent to them. I can also share my own personal experience; no matter how much Jim and I introduced our transgender child to things that aligned with his birth sex, he wasn't having any part of it. As soon as our son, Jordan, was old enough, he made his feelings abundantly clear to us. Initially, we introduced both our young daughters to the same dolls, toys, clothes, and activities and watched how one flourished and one withdrew. Jordan's gender identity was never typical for the female he was assigned at birth and, because we didn't understand he was transgender, the way he was raised presents no possible case for a nurture conclusion.

Looking at the nature side of the argument, the David Reimer case makes perfect sense to people, yet somehow, many negate the same facts when they think of a transgender person. Some people still try to argue that it's not so cut and dry and that social conditioning is the cause of gender dysphoria, which makes no sense to me. Ultimately, in David's case, his gender did align with the sex he was assigned at birth and no amount of social conditioning could change that. With a transgender person like my son, Jordan, it is the complete opposite. His gender identity does not align with his birth sex and yet, still no amount of social conditioning can change that.

To delve deeper into this topic, we will take a look at what science teaches us in the following chapter.

CHAPTER 3

Scientific Discoveries

"It is the glory of God to conceal a matter;
to search out a matter is the glory of kings."
Proverbs 25:2

W hat about the claim that a transgender person has a mental illness that must be treated in a way that retrains the brain? Some suggest you can control the way you think about your gender and learn to be happy with the gender that aligns with the sex you were assigned at birth. Well, if gender dysphoria was merely an illusion, I would stand in agreement with those people. However, there is already too much science pointing to the contrary and undoubtedly far more to be uncovered.

Where can we find proof that transgender people are born transgender and not made that way through social conditioning? While I am certain stronger evidence will continue to present itself as we progress through the 21st and into the 22nd century, there are already some studies we can discuss. In-depth studies on the brain shed some light on how the brain of a transgender person – specifically, those that have a gender identity opposite to their biological sex – differs from that of a non-transgender, or cisgender, person.

Diffusion tensor imaging (DTI) is an MRI imaging technique that, according to a February 2011 study published in the Journal of Psychiatric Research, is the best way to study the grey and white matter in the brain. The study looked at the white brain matter of cisgender males and females, as well as transgender individuals before they had begun any cross-hormone therapy. The idea was to see if the brains of transgender people mirrored more closely to the brains of those with whom they shared a biological sex, or to those with a biological sex opposite to their own – the latter being the biological sex the transgender person identifies with.

The study concluded that the microstructure pattern of the white brain matter in untreated female-to-male transgender people resembled the scans of cisgender males. In layman terms, the scans showed that transgender males – like my son, Jordan, who were born biologically female – had brains that more closely resembled those of biologically born males and *not* of biological females, as many might suspect. Again, the transgender people in the study had not started on any cross-sex hormones, so opposite hormone therapy could not have influenced the results.

There is a region in the brain known as the hypothalamus, which is responsible for sexual behaviour. In 1995, a study done at the Netherlands Institute for Brain Research in Amsterdam examined transsexual brains at autopsy. A detectable difference was discovered that also supports the theory that transgender people are *born* transgender. The study concluded that the brains of male-to-female transsexuals had a hypothalamus similar to those of biological females, and *not* to biological males. Based on these studies, it appears that science supports transgender females and males as having a brain structure that is closer matched to the gender they identify with, rather than their natal sex.

Our natal sex is determined at conception, when the combination of chromosomes sets us up to be either a male, a female, or in some cases, an intersex individual, as we touched on in the first chapter. We have twenty-three sets of chromosomes housed within each of our cells, and each of those chromosomes contains a single DNA module. Our DNA — which consists of four main chemicals: adenine (A), guanine (G), cytosine (C), and thymine (T) — is like a road map for our development.

It holds within it all the instructions needed to build out the proteins we need that carry out the individual functions of our cells; however, cell development can wander from this road map.

If the chemicals that make up our DNA become disturbed in any way, the development of our cells many not develop in the way we expect they should. Our individual cell development can be affected by something called the epigenome. The epigenome is a mix of chemical compounds and proteins that essentially attaches to our DNA and acts like a control switch that can turn on or off our cells. This chemical mix can affect how the trillions of cells in our body develop. For example, it can determine whether or not we are born blind or deaf and whether our bones and tissues form as we expect them to. The smallest environmental changes to the fetus during gestation can cause the epigenome to react in a way that could create a result that lies outside what would be considered typical for our development. This includes gender identity.

If we believe that God created our DNA and the epigenome, then we must also believe God foresaw the variations that could result. Not only did our creator know gender variant people were possible, but one could argue it was expected and perhaps even intentional that a wide variety of non-binary people would be created.

Today, scientists understand barely three percent of our DNA coding. The inner workings of the remaining ninety-seven percent remain unknown. With so much of our DNA still a mystery, I think it is fair to say God knows far more about our creation than we do.

Fetal development is a fascinating and complex process that still leaves much for us to understand. Currently, we can say very little conclusively about our development from a molecular level. However, what we do already know is that the brain begins to develop around seven weeks into a pregnancy and continues to grow and develop up until birth and beyond. A fetus develops genitalia at around eleven weeks, and it is usually fully formed by the twentieth week of pregnancy. In most cases, even though the time periods when the genitalia are developing and the brain is developing are not the same, the genitalia of a baby at birth usually does align with the sex suggested by the baby's chromosome makeup. In some instances, however, this is not the case.

At any time during the gestational period, the delicate chemicals in the developing brain can get disturbed, leaving the door open for a possible disconnect to develop between the gender determined by sex and chromosomes and the gender one self-identifies with in their brain. The fact that gender dysphoria is rare does not mean it does not exist.

Let's look at Alzheimer's as another example of what science can teach us. Scientific discoveries only began to provide us with answers regarding Alzheimer's in the 1980's and 1990's. Before that, we had no information to tell us who might be at risk of developing it. Now, due to discoveries made in the latter part of the twentieth century, we have knowledge about whom, how, and when people may develop Alzheimer's. According to the Alzheimer's Foundation of America, there is a gene, discovered in 1993, called the apolipoprotein E (known as APOE for short), that can tell us if a person is at risk for the disease.

Not only can genes tell us if we are at risk for Alzheimer's, but they can also tell us other information, such as whether early onset is more or less likely. There are two genes – presenilin-1 (PS-1 for short) and presenilin-2 (PS-2 for short) – that point to the possible early onset of Alzheimer's. A gene known as the amyloid precursor protein (APP for short) was discovered in 1987 and points to an inherited form of Alzheimer's.

Alzheimer's affects approximately twenty percent of the population, which is a far greater number than that which represents the transgender community. This explains why science would be allocating funds and research towards studying Alzheimer's. In comparison, studies on gender dysphoria are few and far between. This occurs because it makes sense to focus more resources on what affects more of the population. However, one day, we could discover something just as concrete in gene studies that points to the detection of gender dysphoria.

Society has propelled the transgender story to the foreground in the last few years, but neuroscientists have some catching up to do. What if, one day, it is discovered that transgender people carry a certain gene that cisgender people do not carry, just like the Alzheimer's genes? If there were such a gene, do you think people would be more accepting of transgenderism as an inborn trait? Perhaps, in the future, there will be a gene that will enable us to test children whose behaviour suggests they may have gender dysphoria.

If you are firm in your believe that there is no such thing as a transgender person, or that a transgender person is choosing to feel the way they do, how will you feel if the day comes when we are presented with a gene that points to gender dysphoria? Would this discovery make you think any differently about your attitudes towards the transgender community? How do you expect people on the conservative side of this debate might feel if and when science discovers more evidence to support that transgender people are born transgender?

We, as humans, certainly have a history of treating people we don't understand with spite and contempt. Just look at how we used to treat people with epilepsy. If you were to do a study on the history of the treatment of people with epilepsy, you will find that epileptics have been abused and mistreated. Some were segregated into camps, shocked, forced into ice baths, referred to as "evil witches," subjects of exorcisms, and even denied the right to marry.

It wasn't until the 1850s that a more humane and modern treatment of epilepsy began, through the introduction of the first-generation antiepileptic drug. Since then, modern medicine has evolved and better, more effective drugs have been created. Prescription drugs provide aid to many people with epilepsy by controlling their seizures so they can live normal lives. Today, people with epilepsy can carry on their day-to-day lives without the demeaning and stigmatizing treatment earlier generations had to endure. The passage of time certainly can serve to enlighten us. It seems that with each passing decade, scientific discoveries are advancing more and more rapidly.

The Bible, which was written in a very different time, certainly doesn't hold all the answers. We can look at it for many things, but we must realize that through thousands of years comes knowledge and wisdom that those living back in biblical times just did not have. Society is ever changing, developing, and giving way to new discoveries in medicine, science, and technology that are unlike anything our ancestors could have predicted. In the same way, our children's grandchildren will live in a world we cannot predict.

If you had told my great grandfather I would be walking around with a wireless phone the size of my hand and as thin as a floor tile, he would have thought you were completely nuts. Yet, here we are, in a day where landlines are becoming extinct. And that's only going back a few generations.

There was no knowledge of airplanes or organ transplants two thousand years ago so, looking for references to these things in the Bible would be futile. Similarly, references to gender, as we understand it today, is also absent from biblical text.

There must be weight given to the fact that those who authored the biblical stories that many hold so dear did so without foresight or knowledge of the future. They could only speak to what they understood to be true from their limited perspective at the time.

However, unlike the authors, I believe God did have a foresight that would have shaken the limited minds of the times. I believe, had God told the tales of what the future would hold, it would have been met with widespread disbelief, for how could a mere mortal ever comprehend that which God understands?

Over the last few years, I have had the opportunity to speak with many transgender people, and a common thing that they shared with me was how they prayed to have their gender dysphoria taken away. Many, including my son Jordan, have told me that they would never choose to be a transgender person. Why would they choose a life path that would be so challenging, so ridiculed by others? Why would they choose to place themselves into a minority group that is so harshly judged by others? The truth is they wouldn't.

My son Jordan once told me, before he began his transition, that as difficult as a transgender path would be, the alternative would be impossible for him. He could no more choose to be transgender than he could choose to be left or right handed. Yet, many transgender people suffer an internal struggle that is only intensified by the ridicule of others.

There are many people who may oppose the findings shared in this chapter, no matter how intriguing they are. Admittedly, it is inconceivable for us to know definitively what God's intentions were for our evolution when the first two humans were created. However, it is important for us to acknowledge that the science around gender is still in its infancy. It is impossible for us to predict what science will or will not uncover in the future.

The fact that a transgender identity is biologically based has only begun to be supported and proven by science. Undoubtedly, hidden deep in our genes, there are answers still waiting to be discovered. In the decades ahead, we are sure to have more scientific evidence to evaluate on the topics of sex and gender. As further clinical studies are completed, proof of the hypothesis that gender is an innate characteristic should only become stronger.

Humanity's knowledge is constantly expanding through study and discovery over time, and our religions can benefit greatly from what science teaches us. Who knows what we will understand one hundred years from now? God speaks to those who are willing to listen and sometimes, He speaks through science.

CHAPTER 4

Beliefs Rooted in Religion

"God's spirit is not motionless nor are His words still."
Cheryl B. Evans

There are approximately four thousand different religions around the world and I can't possibly address them all in this book. However, regardless of our faith, much of what we believe and the religion we choose to practice have a lot to do with where we were born in the world. Our interpersonal relationships that had the closest impact to us growing up could also greatly influence our beliefs and attitudes. It is interesting to think about how different our faith might be if we were born in a different part of the world, at a different time, or under wildly different circumstances. It is entirely possible we might have chosen a different religion for ourselves than the one we practice today.

In this book, I would like to focus on the most popular religion based on the percentage of the world's population. The most common religion is Christianity, with over two billion believers and over thirty-one percent of the total population adopting this faith. As I have already shared in the introduction, I consider myself among them, believing in God, Christ, and the Bible as my religious doctrine.

When I think of sex and gender, I imagine the first two people God placed on this earth: Adam and Eve. Genesis 2:4-2:25 of New International Version (NIV) of the Bible tells us in the story of Adam and Eve:

> This is the account of the heavens and the earth when they were created, when the Lord God made the earth and the heavens.
>
> Now no shrub had yet appeared on the earth and no plant had yet sprung up, for the Lord God had not sent rain on the earth and there was no one to work the ground, but streams came up from the earth and watered the whole surface of the ground. Then the Lord God formed a man from the dust of the ground and breathed into his nostrils the breath of life, and the man became a living being.
>
> Now the Lord God had planted a garden in the east, in Eden; and there he put the man he had formed. The Lord God made all kinds of trees grow out of the ground – trees that were

pleasing to the eye and good for food. In the middle of the garden were the tree of life and the tree of the knowledge of good and evil.

A river watering the garden flowed from Eden; from there it was separated into four headwaters. The name of the first is the Pishon; it winds through the entire land of Havilah, where there is gold. (The gold of the land is good; aromatic resin and onyx are also there.) The name of the second river is Gihon; it winds through the entire land of Cush. The name of the third river is Tigris; it runs along the east side of Ashur. And the fourth river is the Euphrates.

The Lord God took the man and put him in the Garden of Eden to work it and take care of it. And the Lord God commanded the man, "You are free to eat from any tree in the garden; but you must not eat from the tree of knowledge of good and evil, for when you eat from it you will certainly die."

Now the Lord God had formed out of the ground all the wild animals and all the birds in the sky. He brought them to the man to see what he would name them; and whatever the man called each living creature, that was its name. So the man gave names to all the livestock, the birds in the sky and all the wild animals.

But for Adam no suitable helper was found. So the Lord God caused the man to fall into a deep sleep; and while he was sleeping, he took one of the man's ribs and then closed up the place with flesh. Then the Lord God made a woman from the rib he had taken out of the man, and he brought her to the man.

The man said, "This is now bone of my bones and flesh of my flesh; she shall be called 'woman,' for she was taken out of man."

That is why a man leaves his father and mother and is united to his wife, and they become one flesh.

Adam and his wife were both naked, and they felt no shame.

Now, that story taken from Genesis seems clear. God first made a male human and then, from him, God created a female human. Many people will conclude from this that God made only two sexes. I've often heard Christians proclaim, "God made only male and female" to dismiss any interpretation to the contrary. They firmly believe that there are only two sexes: male and female. While this statement is true for the initial two humans God created, I don't believe His intention was that there would always only be two sexes in the world.

The problem with the literal interpretation of only two sexes is that we already know that there are babies born intersex, without a simple XX or XY or obvious sexual characteristics. These intersex people do not fall under the sex of male or female. So, there is a third sex — an intersex individual. Therefore, we know we cannot conclude there are only two types of sex within God's creations – man and woman – because to say that would deny the existence of all intersex individuals. What we can say is that the first two humans created – Adam and Eve – appear to be male and female.

My interpretation of God's creation of all things is broad. I don't believe in a narrow-thinking God. I believe God's plan was to intentionally create the wonderfully diverse and enriching world in which we live today. I believe that Adam and Eve were designed with such future diversity in mind, and that they were deliberately encoded with mega genes and the DNA that, through procreation, would separate, divide, and spread, creating a variety of humans. These humans would become people of many races, sexes, and genders. How else could so many different types of people exist? How else could we have so many skin colour variations from the darkest chocolate-brown we see in some people to the palest pink we see in others?

If we are to believe that all humans are descendants of Adam and Eve, then there is no other explanation. We cannot deny that which we know to exist, such as the multitude of races and sexes. This is no different than the way in which God created the animal or plant world. Vast varieties of species and plants emerge, and more and more are being discovered all the time.

It stands to reason that, as people set up in different regions of the world, their gene and chromosome pool would reduce in size. As people procreate with others more like themselves, the population in those areas would grow to reflect that. It makes sense that all the possible variations would have had to have been initially carried by Adam and Eve.

Nowhere in the Bible does it say there is only one race or one type of human, nor does it say that there is no such thing as an intersex or transgender person. The fact that the text neglects to discuss all the different varieties of humans that exist is not the same as saying they don't exist.

I believe all this wonderful variety that we have in the world today was very purposeful on the part of God. There was no intent to divide us by race, nationality, sex, or gender. There was only a wonderful, purposeful creation of the first two human beings, created in such a way that allowed for such a marvelous diversity to exist.

The Bible demands that we love thy neighbour, not love thy neighbour *except* for the ones we don't like. We should think of only one race – the human race – and include everyone as our brothers and sisters. In my interpretation of the Bible, there is no right or wrong way to be human, no right or wrong sex, gender, colour, height, or shape. God must have intended for the multicultural world we live in today. God would have known that not everyone would be born with two arms and two legs, not everyone would be born with an XX or XY chromosomal make-up, and not everyone would have a gender than aligns with their sex.

If being transgender was such a sin, wouldn't it be put into the Ten Commandments? Surely, if it were a sin, it would be considered as serious as "thou shalt not steal." Then again, it is possible that a transgender person is not a sin at all, but rather a purposeful, unique, and wonderful creation of God. In Galatians 3:28, it states, "There is neither Jew nor Gentile, neither slave nor free, nor is there male and female, for you are all one in Christ Jesus."

At the end of the day, an opinion is all each of us has, along with our own interpretation of scripture. No matter how strongly we believe our own interpretations regarding what God's intent was or was not, others will disagree. It is important we recognize this and still try to respect one another.

I was curious about what the interpretation might look like from a pastor's perspective, as someone who is much better versed on the Bible than I am. While I knew it would not likely change the way I saw God, the Bible, and transgender people, I was still curious. I asked Colby Martin, pastor at Sojourn Grace Collective – a progressive Christian Church in San Diego – what he believed the Bible said about transgender people. I'd like to share his response with you:

> The Bible doesn't explicitly address the concept of transgender people. So, right away, it's important to name that, own that, and normalize that. Beyond that, then, I do wonder if we might be able to draw out some other observations that might relate. For instance, when the Bible talks about eunuchs, we (modern minds) typically just think of a castrated male. But in the ancient world, "eunuch" was an umbrella term that was used, yes, to describe a castrated male (known as a "man-made" eunuch), but ALSO, it was used to describe a "natural eunuch." Which was what they called

men who had all the proper biology to procreate, but who, well, just couldn't quite get themselves into it.

With that in mind, when Jesus brings up eunuchs in Matthew 19, he affirms that world view ("some are born that way, some made by man, some choose celibacy"), without criticizing or correcting it. He simply acknowledges that it is hard to accept (which is still true today, isn't it?). But what is REALLY interesting, is in Acts 8 when Philip shares the Good News with the Ethiopian Eunuch and baptizes him into the Way. The Book of Acts is all about the expansive nature of the Table of God — everybody's in, baby. And the early church just kept witnessing as more and more barriers were broken down, and the reality that ALL people are loved by God was setting in. So, what does the Bible say about transgender people? I'm not sure it really does, but it absolutely points to the idea that all people, including the sexual "other," are part of the Family of God.

Colby raises a very important point about inclusiveness with all God's people, reminding us that, in God's eyes, there is not meant to be this separation that modern society often creates. Those that shun or separate others for being human in a way that is different from themselves are, in my opinion, falling short of the type of Christian Jesus would want them to be. Stripping away all our flesh, leaving nothing but our skeletons, shows us that, at the root of it all, none of that matters. Each of us is just as human as the next person.

The Bible tells us in Genesis 1:27, "So God created mankind in his own image, in the image of God he created them; male and female he created them." It does not say "gender fluid" or suggest God's image is anything but male and female. The passage does say he created them male and female and he did. He created Adam as male and Eve as female.

God also intended for the first two humans to go forth and procreate. God, being all-knowing, would have known all the various types of humans Adam and Eve could produce down through the generations. God would have known when He created Adam and Eve that there would be biological things that could occur during gestation that would produce varying outcomes among the world's population. Some children could be born intersex (neither binary male nor female). Some could have certain conditions that result in physical and mental challenges, and one of those challenges could be living with gender dysphoria.

We could go back and erase hundreds of years of progress and say that anyone born with a condition such as gender dysphoria should be fixed. We could say that we considered them subhuman, damaged, or unworthy because that's the way some members of society feel. If we look at the harsh treatment some dole out towards this vulnerable group of people, it does seem that some still feel that way, even today.

If we are to be God-like, is that how God would want us to position ourselves? What about grace and compassion? What about not judging others? Are we to just forget all that? What if the diversity in this world is all part of a test to see if we can follow God's commandment to love thy neighbour? After all, Galatians 5:14 is clear when it says, "For the entire law is fulfilled in keeping this one command: 'Love your neighbor as yourself.'"

Let's go back a step to where the Bible says we are all made in God's image. The Bible never gives a clear description of God in terms of physical appearance, but does use male pronouns and proclaim God as our heavenly Father throughout both the Old and New Testaments. By doing so, we understand God to be male or, at the very least, that male is the way He has chosen to present Himself to humanity.

The lack of physical characteristics also helps us to see God as a wonderfully divine and all-knowing spiritual being. Without humanizing characteristics, we cannot differentiate Him from any other human. Perhaps, there would be even more discrimination in this world if the Bible depicted God as being of a certain race or ethnicity. By leaving out specific physical characteristics of God, the purpose is to not separate us by such earthly things.

We are all children of God, so if we are made in his image, are we not also spiritual beings? As a spiritual being, we don't have the physical characteristics present in our human experience. Gender only comes into play in our human experience. If, in that experience, we are created in God's image, could we not consider our gender to be more fluid, more all-encompassing, and less binary? I believe the Bible supports this theory. When we study scriptures, there are several examples of gender non-binary people.

Let's look at what the Bible says about eunuchs, or the "others". There are members of the human race that are defined in the Bible as neither male nor female, but rather, the sexual others. While the Bible isn't clear-cut in its meaning of eunuchs, it does say that there are multiple ways in which eunuchs come to be.

In Matthew 19:12, the wording in the New International Version states, "For there are eunuchs who were born that way, and there are eunuchs who have been made eunuchs by others and there are those who choose to live like eunuchs for the sake of the kingdom of heaven. The one who can accept this should accept it." Similarly, the English Standard Version of the Bible states, "For there are eunuchs who have been so from birth, and there are eunuchs who have been made eunuchs by men, and there are eunuchs who have made themselves eunuchs for the sake of the kingdom of heaven. Let the one who is able to receive this receive this."

I find the last line very interesting: "Let the one who is able to receive this receive this." Today, there is much resistance to the idea that transgender people are born that way, even intentionally created to be transgender by God Himself. Many people refuse to go there and others, while not completely at odds with the idea, would like more evidence.

It is important for us to consider that, when something is described, even in detail, it is possible that the description can be lacking in information. The Bible provides us with an overview or explanation of many things. That doesn't mean we should conclude those descriptions are all-encompassing. The Bible doesn't list every race, but that omission doesn't mean each one does not exist. Omitting something from a discussion doesn't mean it's not there.

For example, I could tell you there is a box of clothes in the other room. There are shirts, pants, some sweaters, and even a hat or two. If, when you went to look in the box, you found a t-shirt among the other things I described, would you say that t-shirt didn't exist because I failed to mention it? Or would you accept I was explaining something and happened to overlook one type of article?

My point is that, while the Bible doesn't seem to be specific in its mentioning of transgender people, we should not assume that to mean they don't exist. The Bible is no more specific in its mention of intersex people – at least, not in a way we can say conclusively that this or that passage speaks directly to this. Yet, we know intersex people exist and that they are neither male nor female.

In the binary world around us, we see these pink and blue boxes within which we expect everyone to fit. Many Christians would like to believe, or already do believe, in a religious ideology that says people are either male or female. They believe that there is no spectrum or biological instability that would allow for someone with an innate gender identity that is not typically associated with their birth sex. In other words, they want to believe or already believe that there is no way a person can be innately transgender.

Let's look at Psalm 139:13-16.

> For you created my inmost being; you knit me together in my mother's womb. I praise you because I am fearfully and wonderfully made; your works are wonderful, I know that full well. My frame was not hidden from you when I was made in the secret place, when I was woven together in the depths of the earth. Your eyes saw my unformed body; all the days ordained for me were written in your book before one of them came to be.

I've heard many Christians use the above scriptures to support their beliefs that God knew each of us before we were formed. The word "wonderful" speaks to the perfect creation of us as either male or female; God makes no mistakes. I, on the other hand, don't understand this connection. Where does it mention male and female? Where does it talk about the physical appearance at all? To me, all I can interpret from Psalms 139:13-16 is that the creation of the human was purposeful. It was planned, it was wonderful, and it was hidden and created in the mother's womb.

This could easily be interpreted to mean each human is uniquely wonderful in their design. It could be saying that even those born with mental or physical challenges have been specifically planned and designed that way. God knew that which He was creating, but we are offered no specific description of that creation. It could very well be a person without legs, a person who is blind or deaf. It could even be a person who has the brain of one gender and the physical body of another – the person could be born any number of ways. What we know for certain is that the baby is birthed from the mother's womb, it's fearfully and wonderfully made, and planned by God, who knew us before our own mother knew us. There is nothing mentioned about sex or gender in that passage.

We have not made it easy for a non-binary person to feel accepted. The entire idea of binary genders doesn't feel like an expectation put on us by God, but rather, some human construct that society has created. What's worse is that this society that we have constructed, with all its imperfections and hierarchies, is failing to acknowledge that the different races and genders were all purposely created by God. This leaves the most vulnerable among us to fight for equal rights and freedoms which should be the birthright of ALL of God's children.

Isaiah 56:4-5 states: "For this is what the Lord says: To the eunuchs who keep my Sabbaths, who choose what pleases me and hold fast to my covenant — to them I will give within my temple and its walls a memorial and a name better than sons and daughters; I will give them an everlasting name that will endure forever."

What is most interesting about this passage from Isaiah is that it shows us how the biblical text is evolving, and how what once was rejected is now accepted. This cancels out the stance taken earlier in Deuteronomy 23, where eunuchs and foreigners were excluded from the assembly or worship gathering.

Isaiah 56:4-5 suggests that people, who are different, even considered outcasts by some, are not outcasts to the Lord. They are not judged by what makes them different. They are not excluded because they are "others". They are included because the only thing that matters to the Lord is that they are willing to do what pleases Him, keep His covenant and the sabbaths. Another example of inclusiveness rather than division, emphasizing once again, is the importance God places on loving thy neighbour. There is no effort on God's part to separate people based on their differences.

Today, however some Christians are quick to point out the differences in people, their gender variance specifically, and make them feel as outcasts. They disregard God's desire for inclusivity and acceptance among us. They decide to become judge and jury for things like gender, when scripture seems to support God was accepting and affirming of all people, even those falling outside of the gender binary.

Perhaps the everlasting name that was to be given to the eunuchs was the word *transgender.* This modern-day word does seem fitting in the way it acts as an umbrella term for many gender-variant people, bringing them all together in an accepting and inclusive way.

Who are we to say the journey that God has chosen for us is wrong? Who are we to suggest we know more than God, who created the heavens and the earth? If God created Adam and Eve with all the necessary genes and chromosomes so that such diversity among His children exists, who are we to question that? If someone is born with gender dysphoria and the transgender path is the journey God has chosen for them, then who are we to question that? The variety seen among all God's children is vast and beautiful and completely intentional. Let us not forget that God is non-binary, for He is the Father, the Son, and the Holy Spirit.

Jesus was a carpenter. What do you suppose Jesus would have said to a transgender person that had asked him to build a table for them? I believe Jesus would have built them the table and that he would have taken the same care and attention he would have taken if he were building it for a cisgender person. Once the table was built, it would be very much in keeping with Jesus' demeanour to sit and partake in a meal with the transgender person for whom he built the table. I certainly don't feel it would have been like Jesus to deny a transgender person service.

The fact that, today, so many are denying service to the LGBTQ community and are using the Bible or the Christian religion as a reason for their decision seems to be un-Christ-like behaviour. Nevertheless, it is how some people conduct themselves or their businesses, and the reason why is steeped in years and years of religious dogma. If Jesus were to have a shop, the sign on the door would say everyone was welcome. Don't you agree?

Then, there are those who consider themselves to be atheists, neither believing in Jesus nor God. Sometimes, I think they do a better job showing kindness and compassion towards others than some Christians do. In fact, without the conflict of a religion or fear of God, atheists are free to accept and love everyone without judgement or discrimination. Theoretically, we are all free to love without judgement and discrimination; we just don't all chose to do so.

When you think of who exactly are casting out those that are different, it's not atheists that you hear about. Rather, it's usually Christians, and other strong religious people. It seems more often than not, the ones who believe in God and Jesus are the ones acting in inhospitable ways, even towards their own children and families. I can't recall any instances where I have heard or read about an atheist throwing their children out for being LGBTQ, but I do hear about it happening all the time from religious-based homes. I can't believe Jesus would encourage any parent to throw out their own child simply for being LGBTQ. Can you?

Granted, there are many loving Christian families who both affirm and accept their LBGTQ children, but that doesn't bring solace to those children who aren't as fortunate.

CHAPTER 5

Living Life According to The Bible

"Who is wise and understanding among you?
Let them show it by their good life,
by deeds done in the humility that comes from wisdom."
James 3:13

People will say they live their life according to the Bible all the time. What they really should be saying is they live their life according to *their interpretation* of the Bible. There's a big difference between the two, and the intended meaning of something can easily get lost in translation. Multiple people can read the same text, and yet, interpret it in different ways.

I am not just referring to biblical text. Heck, this happens with modern-day texting. You text a note to a friend and they text back something that clearly tells you they misunderstood the meaning of your original text message. When we look at biblical text and interpret it differently, how do we prove beyond the shadow of a doubt which interpretation is the correct one? In the current day, news and issues can be confusing and mistakes can be made in the way we interpret information. It is only reasonable that it would be easier, not harder, to misinterpret information when the times, issues, and people we are discussing are from thousands of years ago.

At some point, can we not all set our pride aside and accept that there are some things we may never know for certain – at least, not in this lifetime? Most of us can admit that. Although we may think we know what another person is thinking, it is impossible to know the thoughts of another person for certain. As intelligent beings ourselves, we should be able to admit that we have no right to claim we know the intention of God.

In many instances, we teach what we were taught. The teachings of each church and/or religion are being passed down through the generations like a great family tradition. The church and its elders teach their congregations the interpretations of the scriptures as they understand them or as they have been instructed to teach them. This establishes an understanding and belief within their followers. These interpretations then go from church to home, where believers continue to pass these interpretations on to their own children.

It continues this way generation after generation. People continue to share scripture in the way it has been represented to and accepted by them without ever stopping to question that, perhaps, what they are passing down is not the interpretation they should be following. They do this blindly, without question, because it is and always has been the way they have been taught.

There was a story about a granddaughter who always cut the ends of the roast before she put it in the pan. One day, her husband asked her why she did that every time she made roast beef and she shrugged and said, "I don't know. It's just the way my mother showed me and what my mother has always done."

"But why?" asked the husband.

The wife, unable to answer, phoned her mother and asked her. "Mom why did you teach me to always cut off the end of the roast before I cook it?" Her mother admitted she didn't know and explained to her daughter it was the way she was taught by her mother. The granddaughter, now curious for an answer, called her grandmother and asked her about why it was important to cut the ends off the roast.

The grandmother began to laugh and said, "I didn't do it for any other reason than to get the roast to fit into my pan."

When we learn something – especially something that has passed down from people we trust – we reason that it must be good information that has already been vetted and proven through the ages. We go with it, accept it, use it, and pass it on again. We should not blindly follow others without understanding for ourselves why such traditions exist. People before us have passed down interpretations of the scriptures for thousands of years. That doesn't mean we should continue to do so without thoughtful, careful consideration of what it says, even if what we discover is far from what we have always been taught.

Debates are healthy when we can have them in a non-confrontational and non-judgmental way, or when we can speak calmly and rationally about topics we are passionate about. This is what I have tried to do throughout this book. There are other books on the market that will further support some of the arguments I have put forth, as well as some that will dispute my conclusions. I am grateful for these books because it allows us to explore ideas and use the brains which God has given us to think for ourselves, weigh the evidence, and interpret and draw our own conclusions. In doing so, let's just remember everyone has the right to their own interpretation of the Bible and we should respect each other's rights to those interpretations, even if we don't agree with them.

Today, we can witness the contempt the Christian church has for transgender people beginning to soften, which is not unlike their earlier contempt for the Jewish people. We are seeing an upheaval in the way Christians interpret the scriptures as they relate to transgender people, but there is still much work to be done. Every day, transgender people are being discriminated against, beaten, and even killed unjustly in the name of God. The level of hatred some people possess for this vulnerable community is disturbing and unwarranted. Children are being treated as outcasts and thrown out of their homes – all in the name of Christianity.

Aren't you worried about the afterlife? I've had people ask me that question, all the while telling me that, by allowing my child to transition, I must not be concerned with having eternal life. Now, who's mind reading? This presumes two things: first, that I agree that there is something to worry about – which I do not – and second, that God will not allow me or my son into heaven because I have affirmed him as a transgender person and assisted him with his transition.

Suggesting that I am not worried about the afterlife is a smug and backhanded comment, but one that I lose no sleep over. It's just another instance of someone using God to shame or bully another person, and I try very hard to ignore the bullies. As far as my son goes, I choose to love him unconditionally, just as I do his cisgender sister. I don't believe anyone will be turned away from heaven for having loved another unconditionally.

The younger generation today seems to have more compassion for those that are different. While not inclusive to all of that generation, it does appear many are doing a much better job of embracing diversity than their elders. Should this pattern continue, we should see a continued move towards a more Christ-like acceptance of transgender people within the church.

One consideration is that if people don't see their churches as safe, accepting, and inclusive places, fewer may embrace the church altogether. I know of many families who have chosen to leave their church because it became clear to them that they or a member of their family were not accepted or tolerated for being LGBTQ. Though churches can be a wonderful place of community, if they treat others as outcasts, more and more people may choose to worship elsewhere. After all, God's spirit is not confined to the man-made establishment of the church and the church is not needed in order to feel close to God.

CHAPTER 6

True Faith vs. Blind Faith

"For we live by faith not by sight."
2 Corinthians 5:7

How can we know that the faith we have is true faith and not blind faith? After all, if the best theologians of our time can disagree on their interpretations of the Bible, how are we to know that the truth we hold onto, as a part of our own faith, is the truth? Many theologians have made it their life's purpose to study and ascertain the true meaning of the scriptures, so it should come as no surprise that the average person may view scripture differently.

Disunity among the churches is not uncommon today, as congregations are being taught completely different things about the exact same scriptures. No wonder there is so much agitation, even among fellow Christians. The different ways in which we personally interpret scripture flow down from everything that we have been taught about it. Our understanding is influenced by the way in which we are taught, as well as by the person doing the teaching. What is our relationship to our teachers? Are they persons we respect and believe wholeheartedly? What is the full level of influence our teachers have on us? Are they our parents, our ministers, or other highly trusted advocates?

There comes a time when each object is given a name. There was a time when someone decided a pot should be called a pot, and a house should be called a house. We no longer question the name of such objects, but instead, accept that these are the correct names and we continue to refer to these objects by these names. There is no conflict or inherent damage that can be caused to an innate object, even if we do mislabel it.

However, with real people, our misnaming has the capacity to do real harm. A transgender person feels real pain when they have been misnamed or misgendered. There is a real suffering that we don't need to think about when dealing with innate objects. For this reason, more care should be given before anyone cements themselves into a faith that suggests transgender people are against God.

There are times when it may be appropriate to just take things at face value, without ever questioning or challenging it, but is that how we should be with our faith? Should we not ensure – if not just for the sake of our fellow man, but for ourselves – that our faith is based on truth? Do we really want someone else to tell us what our faith should look like, act like, and label it for us? With blind faith, even a falsehood can be accepted as truth if delivered with enough conviction, authority, persistence, and persuasion.

The difference between true faith and blind faith is that with blind faith, we are allowing others to decide or dictate what we should believe, how we feel about it, and what is true for us without questioning the validity of that faith. True faith only comes after we have examined, scrutinized, doubted, challenged, questioned, and credited or discredited the very faith which we have been taught. True faith is believing what you believe because it is *your* belief, not what you have been taught to believe. True faith is not easy; it requires work and dedication.

When we set out to challenge or question that which has been taught to us about the scriptures, it can be met with resistance from our teachers. We can be told it is not our place to question – that we are not qualified to know what those in authority know. We can come up against widespread disapproval, and may even feel at risk of losing our church communities, loved ones, or teachers if we persist. Biblical messages can be difficult to discern and many seem unfinished, unclear, and almost purposely ambiguous. But if we are to have faith in these messages, should we not question and challenge them for ourselves, rather than blindly follow the teachings of another?

Is it enough to say we believe in the Bible because it is the word of God? How do we know that it is the word of God? Is that word not only as good as our interpretation of it? After all, it is full of inconsistencies. Take, for example, in John 19:17, where we are told Jesus carried his own cross: "Carrying his own cross, he went out to the place of the Skull (which in Aramaic is called Golgotha)." But in Mark 15:21-22, we are told a man called Simon carried the cross: "A certain man from Cyrene, Simon, the father of Alexander and Rufus, was passing by on his way in from the country, and they forced him to carry the cross. They brought Jesus to the place called Golgotha (which means 'the place of the skull')." Which story is true and which is false? Did John or Mark speak truth?

What about the contradictions surrounding the Resurrection itself? In Mark, we are told that women arrived at the tomb at the rising of the sun, but John tells us it was dark when the women arrived. In Luke, we are told the tomb itself was open, but in Matthew, it says the tomb was closed. Which stories are true and which are false?

With such clear incongruities, we can only conclude that the Bible is filled with false statements because, when there is a contradiction such as these, both statements cannot be correct. These types of inconsistencies begin at the very beginning in Genesis, where scriptures contradict the order in which the first woman and the animals were made following the creation of man, and become a reoccurring theme throughout both the Old and New Testaments.

There should be no surprise here, as people get their stories mixed up all the time. The unreliability of human recollection has been demonstrated throughout history. In fact, children make a game of it called "broken telephone," and laugh at how distorted their messages become from the first person through the last in the chain.

Knowing such contradictions exist in the Bible, you would think it would remind us all to be careful regarding the weight we place on any one passage. Some might argue that the inconsistencies are unimportant and won't impede our understanding of the overall message, but I would disagree. It matters quite a bit, and especially to those that cherry-pick which passages they are going to use as fuel to defend their positions or to discredit the position of another.

Our past has taught us we have not always been good at interpreting the Bible. Think about the cruelty brought down on the Jewish people from the Christian churches, who claimed the scriptures depicted the Jewish people as evil and killers of Christ. Decades ago, Christians hated and feared the Jewish people, claiming scriptures like Matthew 27:25 and John 8:44 showed their hatred and fear were justified.

Martin Luther wrote a paper in 1543 entitled "On the Jews and their lies," which encouraged disdain towards the Jewish community. He stated in his paper that "Jewish synagogues and schools should be set on fire," and then, went on to say, "they should be shown no mercy or kindness and that 'We' are at fault for not slaying them." Churches then taught this to their congregations and found support for their positions in the biblical text.

Thankfully, we have come a long way since then. Many of us are too young to even remember the level of hatred Protestants and Catholics had toward the Jewish people. Today, the scriptures used against our Jewish brothers and sisters have been reinterpreted and Christians widely accept the Jewish people as having a coveted place among all of God's children. We are no longer wrongful accusers of the Jewish people, but rather, strong allies and friends. We look to their sacred texts to help deepen our own understandings and aid us in advancing and perfecting our own teachings.

Looking back, we see how terribly unjust it was to use scripture to uphold slavery and white supremacy. For decades, the Bible was used to suggest blacks were a lesser race than whites and that they could be bought and sold as slaves. Centuries later, we can still see an ugly prejudice that remains among some whites. Some say they are not prejudiced, but their subtle and hurtful actions still say otherwise. The Ku Klux Klan — or KKK, as they are commonly known — remains the most hateful organized group that still terrorizes African Americans to this day.

Thankfully, while the majority of white Christians realize how outrageous and lacking of substantive evidence and merit the justification for slavery was, the deep-seated pain they unleashed lingers. Horrible injustices poured down on an entire race because white Christians had wrongly interpreted the scriptures and so unyieldingly taught their followers that slavery was just. This message was so strong that it reached beyond the church and imprinted itself on atheists, as well.

When we consider the lessons we have learned from our past with regards to our previous misinterpretations of scripture about African Americans and the Jewish people, can we also consider that many Christians might be making similar mistakes with regards to the scriptures and LGBTQ people?

While views in some churches are beginning to soften and people are already looking at interpreting the scriptures differently, many more are still teaching their congregations to openly reject LGBTQ people. They teach their parishioners that lesbians, gays, bisexual, and transgender people are morally inferior and will be denied entrance to heaven. Other churches will welcome LGBTQ people into their church community; some even going so far as to stipulate they must agree to leave behind their LGBTQ "lifestyle"; some welcome them in the hopes that they might "save" them.

Then, there are the churches that hold themselves out as LGBTQ-affirming churches. There is a huge difference between churches that are welcoming and those that are affirming. Churches that are welcoming will accept LGBTQ people into their church communities. Churches that say they are welcoming do so, stopping short of affirming LGBTQ people. Churches that welcome but don't affirm still hold the belief that LGBTQ people are choosing to live a sinful lifestyle and that they are going against God.

Whereas, the churches that say they are affirming of LGBTQ people are saying that they do not believe that being lesbian, gay, bisexual, transgender, or queer is a sin. Affirming churches hold the belief that LGBTQ people are created that way by God and the way they live their life is not a lifestyle choice they are making. If you or someone you love is LGBTQ and looking to belong to a church, you may want to seek out one that is openly affirming, rather than simply welcoming.

The Bible calls for us to help the homeless and to feed and care for them. Ironically, religious disdain for the LGBTQ is contributing to a surprisingly high percentage of the homeless population. In some major cities, LGBTQ people make up a huge percentage of the homeless, often approaching 30-40%. More surprising still is that these people are often youth who were not only rejected by their church communities, but by the very homes in which they should have had safety and security. Discrimination taught in the church and carried into the home leaves many LGBTQ youth to be rejected by their families and put out of their own homes. Religious barriers go beyond the walls of the church, invading our homes, workplaces, and social gathering places. These barriers are unthreatening towards non-LGBTQ, yet hostile to lesbians, gays, bisexuals, transgender, and queer persons.

There is an important distinction with regards to the parents who turn away from their children by putting them out on the street or those who place them into foster care, which sadly, is a reality for some transgender children. The distinction is that many of these parents are not inherently bad parents – they just don't see any other way to handle it. It is difficult not to judge them, but we must try to understand the extent to which their religious teachings have enveloped their whole being. Many of these parents have grown up immersed in anti-LGBTQ teachings, which have been passed down through the generations. It has been ingrained in them and become a trusted part of their faith. Whether or not you agree with that doesn't negate the fact that these teachings have shaped them into the people they have become.

Some of these parents feel they have no choice and believe they must not go against these teachings. The anti-LGBTQ interpretation of scripture has been taught for far too long. It has caused good parents to fear going against what they believe God teaches. They may even fear that, by going against God, they will be denied access to heaven. Believing their own children will not experience the afterlife is painful for these parents. They continue to embrace what they have been taught with such conviction that, even as their own families are being destroyed, they believe they are living their life faithfully to God. Looking to their faith and teachings, they feel justified in their decision to reject the gender identity of their own children.

While I don't understand their stance, nor do I wish to make light of the harm that is coming to the children that are ostracized from their homes, I do have compassion for what their families must endure. I do wish to acknowledge the power religious teachings can have and the way that specifically anti-LGBTQ teachings have gravely affected LGBTQ children and the LGBTQ community.

We talk about the gender boxes society has erected — the blue box for boys and the pink box for girls — but often negate to discuss the boxes our religion puts us in. Each religion has strong fundamental beliefs that followers are expected to believe, should they desire inclusion with the group. There is little room to maneuver in these religious boxes. Stepping outside of them or challenging their walls is unacceptable and frowned upon by most religious communities. But, at some point, we need to open the religious box, and allow for not only others to come in, but ourselves to expand beyond its restrictive space.

Just as God is alive, moving, and expanding in our lives, so should we be. We should embrace new discoveries and appreciate the valuable lessons past religious mistakes have taught us. There should be no fear in growing spiritually, in reevaluating our previous thinking. Spiritual growth should comfort us, build our confidence, and even inspire us to be better Christians.

Showing hostility and contempt towards one another will not bring us closer to God. But, if we choose to build harmony, if we work at building bridges between us, we can provide a valued contribution to humanity while simultaneously serving God. God is about inclusion, not division. We can't possibly be one with Him until we can be one with all His children.

Our thoughts and feelings around transgender people — and perhaps, by extension, all members of the LGBTQ community — may not be easily challenged or changed. Our own upbringing, life influences, and experiences have shaped our individual core beliefs. It is through these core beliefs that we view the world, others, and even ourselves. So, depending on where you stood before picking up this book, it's unlikely your beliefs about transgender people have changed radically. Sure, they may have softened if you were coming to this topic with no prior knowledge on the subject, but you likely are still being pulled towards your original beliefs.

Often, when presented with information that is contrary to our core beliefs, we become naturally defensive, even more rigid. This is because it is hard for us to imagine that something about our beliefs could be flawed. When our beliefs shift, everything around us shifts; our attitudes, thoughts, and expectations for the future are all influenced. For this reason, I hope we can all be compassionate and even extend some grace and patience to those who hold a strong opposing position to our own — even though doing so will not change the undeniable fact that life for LGBTQ people is still far more difficult that it should be.

While it may take far longer than I would personally like it to, I think we are moving in the right direction. Walls are beginning to crumble and more and more people are revisiting the scriptures with a genuine desire to find truth. More people are open to whatever they find, whether it affirms or refutes what they had previously been taught. It is not easy to admit the teachings around which our faith has been built might be flawed. It takes courage to evaluate scripture you are so certain about, but it is all about having *true* faith.

The direction today seems to be moving toward greater acceptance and inclusion for LGBTQ people in the church. While the United Church of Christ and others have already taken an affirming position, the hope is more churches will follow and eventually, replace anti-LGBTQ teachings altogether.

I will continue to hold onto my personal belief that

– in the end – we will all decide to have true faith when drawing our own conclusions about what the Bible *really* says about transgender people and the rest of the LGBTQ community.

CHAPTER 7

What About Culture?

*"Therefore you are to be perfect, as
your heavenly Father is perfect."*
Matthew 5:48

W hat does culture have to do with it? What
about our culture makes it easier or harder to
accept transgender people as an equal gender
to the binary genders of male and female? Culture has
a great deal to do with it. Our culture dictates much of
what we, as individuals, believe about gender. Whether
or not we believe it is perfectly okay to express our
gender in non-conforming ways is often dictated by the
values, principles, and beliefs of the culture in which we
live.

In modern culture, when we talk about a boy or
a man, most people assumed that we were speaking
about a biological male. When we are speaking about
a girl or woman, most people assume we are speaking
about a biological female. Most people don't think of a

transgender woman as *just* a woman or a transgender man as *just* a man. Our culture in North America still thinks of gender as being binary. However, there are cultures that incorporate a transgender narrative into their understanding of gender that goes beyond what many Christians in North America would be comfortable with.

In parts of South Asia, including India and Pakistan, they recognize a third gender. This third gender is not only culturally acknowledged, but recognized by the government, as well. This third gender is known in their culture as *hijra.* They are feminine persons who were either born intersex or biologically male. Some have been castrated and others maintain the genitalia they had a birth. They have a strong female gender expression and would be recognized in North America as transgender women.

In Navajo culture, they recognize four separate and distinctive genders. The first two are the binary genders widely recognized among western culture, that being the cisgender male and cisgender female, though the Navajo simply refer to them as male and female. In addition to those individuals, they also have what they consider two-spirited people. These individuals make up the other two of their four recognized genders.

The first is the biologically born female who lives life from childhood into adulthood guided by the male spirit within, and is recognized as being more masculine than feminine. The fourth gender is the biologically born male who lives from childhood into adulthood guided by the female spirit within, and is recognized as being more feminine than masculine. All four of these genders are considered natural, inborn genders and all are fully accepted in Navajo culture.

The Navajos' belief in four genders aligns with our modern-day narrative of cis male, cis female, transgender male, and transgender female. Their spiritual and religious beliefs vary among their culture, just as ours do. Some, but not all, Navajos consider themselves Christians, and those that recognize a higher being may refer to Him as God or The Great Spirit.

There are also cultures that insist on strict gender roles for their people and condemn or punish those for stepping outside of what is culturally acceptable for a male or female. For transgender people living in these cultures, they feel like they have no alternative but to suffer in silence. The sheer act of admitting their gender dysphoria or attempting to seek help for it may cause them to meet a fate far worse than they may already be suffering.

Some cultures make schooling for females difficult, if not impossible, and in some countries, women are not permitted to vote or to drive. In some cultures, women are the property of their husbands and dare not go against him. These suppressive cultures seem so completely opposite to what the women in the western world experience today. I say *today* because it wasn't that many decades ago that similar restrictions were placed on woman here in North America. If it were not for the valiant efforts of women like Elizabeth Cady Stanton, Lucretia Mott and Susan B. Anthony, we may still be fighting for the woman's right to vote.

Pioneering the way for the transgender community were brave transgender women like Roberta Cowell, born in 1918, who in the early 1950's became the first known British transgender woman to undergo sex reassignment surgery. Cowell was a fighter pilot in the Second World War, as well as a race car driver.

Then, there is Christine Jordensen, who was born in 1926. Jordensen was first person widely known in the United States to have transitioned. Coincidentally, Jordensen also served in World War II and also underwent sex reassignment surgery in the early 1950's.

Reed Erickson was a philanthropist who contributed millions of dollars to the LGBTQ movement from the mid-sixties through the mid-eighties. Erickson lived from 1917 to 1992 and was a transgender man who transitioned during the 1960's. He devoted much of his professional life to education and support of the transgender community.

Today, there are other names we recognize like Caitlyn Jenner, Jazz Jennings, Gavin Grimm, and Chaz Bono, who all have helped to shed light on the topic of transgenderism. As controversial as the subject of transgenderism is, these individuals have helped to open some minds — as well as some hearts — and moved the conversation forward. Regardless of the times or the culture, transgender people have always been here. It is just that today, through advances in technology and the media, their stories and messages are more readily known.

In general, men have culturally been expected to be the stronger sex and, because of this, society often puts pressure on males from a very early age to act a certain way. Little boys are told they can't cry or that they should "man up." Boys are discouraged from playing with dolls or practicing dance because to partake in such activities would be construed as unacceptable female behaviour. They are conditioned to be stronger and, in many cultures, superior to their female counterparts. Men are expected to be decisive, dominant, independent, and logical, where women are expected to be ruled more by their emotions than logic. They are expected to be passive, non-aggressive, caring, and nurturing. The concept of a working mother and a stay-at-home dad is not one that many cultures are willing to embrace.

Thankfully, here in North America and in most of Europe, the attitudes around gender roles are not as restrictive as they once were. Today, men and women have the freedom to explore many occupations and both are free to go after the same goals and aspirations. So, you can see culture plays a huge role in how we perceive gender and how we expect certain people to behave. While gender itself may not be socially constructed, gender expectations certainly are.

Now, go back thousands of years to what culture must have been like in biblical times. It would be vastly different than today, and expecting anyone who lived during that time to understand and speak to what we would be experiencing today would be impossible. Our understanding of human sexuality and gender are far more advanced and we push against the restrictive understandings of our past because we have evolved. We have wisdom today that is incomparable to the past. From our enlightened position, we can see the depths of gender like no generation before us has experienced.

Slow and steady, like a turtle, society begins to move in the direction of change. We evolve and adapt to more modern-day times. We become aware, open, even more willing to accept the things we once never understood. Granted, we have a long way to go. While I want to recognize the progress we have made, I don't want to suggest that our evolution is anywhere near complete. If it were we wouldn't continue to see transgender people beaten and murdered just for being who they are. Though many continue to let hate and intolerance rule their actions, there are many more who are now embracing ideas which they once stood firmly against; they are beginning to stand beside others in their fight for equality, dignity, and mercy.

Today, many Christians are looking at scripture through a fresh lens, one that offers a wider view on humanity. With consideration of the culture in which we live today and new knowledge about transgender people, we can give birth to a new understanding — an understanding that not only aligns with scripture, but perhaps more importantly, aligns with how God would want us to comprehend gender.

We learn from brave young people like Gavin Grimm. He is a transgender teenager from Virginia that stood bravely and addressed the Superior Court in 2017 to fight for the rights of transgender people. Grimm's fight began when his high school refused him access to the boys' bathroom and the school board supported the school's decision. The case was known as *G.G v. Gloucester School Board.* While, at the time of this writing, Grimm has not yet found the justice he seeks, he is elevating the stage.

Even though Grimm's case was pushed back from The United States Supreme Court in March of 2017, it was acknowledged by Senior Judge Andre Davis of the United States Court of Appeal for the fourth circuit, who wrote a thoughtful and detailed Order outlining his thoughts surrounding the fight Grimm was putting forth. In it, he spoke of the bravery Grimm had and his own disdain for the way society treats the transgender community. He called them "a vulnerable group that has traditionally been unrecognized, unrepresented, and unprotected."

Judge Davis also acknowledged in his order how "G.G.'s plight has shown us the inequities that arise when the government organizes society by outdated constructs like biological sex and gender. Fortunately, the law eventually catches up to the lived facts of people."

Finally, in closing, Judge Davis added the poem "Famous" by Naomi Shehab Nye. Before its inclusion Davis shared: "G.G. is and will be famous, and justifiably so. But he is not "famous" in the hollowed-out Hollywood sense of the term. He is famous for the reasons celebrated by the renowned Palestinian-American poet Naomi Shehab Nye, in her extraordinary poem, *Famous*. Despite his youth and the formidable power of those arrayed against him at every stage of these proceedings, "[he] never forgot what [he] could do."":

> *The river is famous to the fish.*
>
> *The loud voice is famous to silence,*
> *which knew it would inherit the earth*
> *before anybody said so.*
>
> *The cat sleeping on the fence is famous to the birds*
> *watching him from the birdhouse*
>
> *The tear is famous, briefly, to the cheek.*
>
> *The idea you carry close to your bosom*
> *is famous to your bosom.*
>
> *The boot is famous to the earth,*
> *more famous than the dress shoe,*
> *which is famous only to floors.*
>
> *The bent photograph is famous to the one who*

carries it and not at all famous to the one who is
pictured.

I want to be famous to shuffling men
who smile while crossing streets,
sticky children in grocery lines,
famous as the one who smiled back.

I want to be famous in the way a pulley is famous,
or a buttonhole, not because it did anything
spectacular, but because it never forgot what it
could do.

The poem *Famous* was a most interesting inclusion by Davis. In this poem by Naomi Shehab Nye, she eloquently communicates the relationship between fame and the thing by which fame is attained. It's almost as if Davis's inclusion of this poem is saying that Grimm's plight shouldn't be a debate, nor should it be something that requires a fight at all.
Davis further stated:

Today, G.G. adds his name to the list of plaintiffs whose struggle for justice has been delayed and rebuffed; as Dr. King reminded us, however, "the arc of the moral universe is long, but it bends toward justice." G.G.'s journey may be delayed or, given he has since graduated from high school, the baton may be passing to others. Either way it is a fight that is not yet finished.

Grimm's case is an important one for the transgender community because it challenges society to think differently about gender identity and how our culture attempts to box people into the binaries around sex and gender. It seems from Judge Davis's remarks that he values the advances we as a culture have made in our understanding and acceptance of transgender people, while communicating that we still have a long way to go.

Granted, not everyone will agree with Judge Davis. Not everyone embraces the modern-day understandings of sexuality and gender, and that is why we are having this conversation. I do not believe there is an inherently wrong way to express gender. It is up to each of us to decide for ourselves what gender means to us and to express it in the way that feels right for us and us alone. Our life experience is best lived as the person we know ourselves to be – our authentic self – not the gender or gender role anyone else feels best suits us.

If you are a woman who wants to be CEO of a big corporation rather than a stay-at-home mom, I say, go for it. If you are a man who would rather take care of your kids and cook for your family than work outside the home, all the power to you. It's called your life for a reason.

If you are a transgender man or woman and are truly happy living life opposite to your biological sex, I say great. If you feel more gender fluid, and believe your gender falls somewhere else along the gender spectrum, you should not let others question the validity of your own gender identity. Ignore societal binary boxes and the cultural stigma that exists around gender and just be happy – just be you (provided of course, that you do not reside in a part of the world where your personal safety would be at great risk to do so).

Sometimes, if we want our culture to move in a particular direction, we need to be prepared to stand up for what matters most to us. Cultures can evolve more quickly when the people in them collaborate, share, and help educate one another.

CHAPTER 8

Coming Out

"So do not fear, for I am with you; do not be dismayed,
for I am your God. I will strengthen you
and help you; I will uphold you with my
righteous right hand."
Isaiah 41:10

Why do some people wait so long to come out? If they were born transgender, wouldn't they all come out as youngsters? Some transgender people don't declare their gender as different from their biological sex when their gender dysphoria first presents itself to them. For those that don't vocalize their gender dysphoria, there can be varying reasons. Some hold back out of uncertainty, some out of fear, some to avoid the stigma others may place on them, and some for reasons we may never understand.

In all cases, coming out can be a heart-wrenching and difficult decision with many factors to consider – not the least of which could be their personal safety.

Whatever the reason someone has for waiting years, even decades to come out as a transgender person, it does not in any way suggest that they were not always transgender.

One of the biggest misconceptions about transgender people is that it's a choice and that they just wake up one day and decide they would like to give a go at being the opposite sex. Gender runs deep; while it is an innate characteristic of a person, for those whose gender differs from that which society expects, it is anything but simple. It takes great courage for a transgender person to come out to others, yet somehow, we neglect to acknowledge this. Instead, society is quick to judge, to criticize, and even dehumanize these brave individuals.

The first person that usually tells us what gender we are is our parent or primary caregiver. They speak to us after we are born, using gender specific pronouns and saying things like, "what a cute little boy you are," or, "what a beautiful little girl you are." Our natural instinct is to trust the words of our parent or primary caregiver, so we rationalize that we are the gender we are being told we are. Why would we, as babies and young children, have a reason to think otherwise?

Our parents are our first teachers – they teach us the names of our body parts as they point to our toes, saying, "toes," to our hands, arms, legs, and so on. We discover so much about our own bodies through early teachings of our parents – long before we even go to school. They speak the truth to us about these things. These same people tell us the sky is blue, and it is. They tell us water is wet and that is also true, so it stands to reason we would believe we are the boy or girl we are being told we are.

The struggle comes when a transgender person's brain feels conflict with the understanding of what they have been taught throughout their lives. I often think back to the language Jordan used when he first vocalized his gender dysphoria to me. He was about three or four then, and I had never heard of transgender children at the time, so I had no idea that this could be anything like that. Jordan didn't tell me he was a boy. Why would he? He trusted me – as an authority figure and his mom. I had always told him the truth. I had always told him he was a girl.

What he said was, "I feel like a boy and I want to be a boy," and "Why am I not a boy?" Even at such a young age, Jordan was intelligent and rational in his proclamation to me – I was just listening from a place of pure ignorance.

I had this idea about kids believing what they are told without a doubt when I watched a cute video that was floating around social media recently. It was of two little girls, one of whom was telling a little boy (they all looked about three or four years of age) that it was raining outside. The little boy told the little girl it was not raining outside – it was spitting. The little girl argued back that she knew it was raining because her mother told her it was. The little boy, getting frustrated, firmly replied that his mother said it was spitting. This exchange went back and forth a few times, with both children getting firmer and firmer in their stance, yet neither of them realizing that they were both correct. They were both telling the other it was doing the same thing; they just didn't realize the words they were using meant the same thing. It was quite adorable.

The point is that we instill knowledge in children and they soak it up like little sponges, without ever doubting its validity. So, when a transgender child feels like a boy and a parent has told him as far back as he can remember that he is a girl, what is the child to think? It should not be surprising that these transgender children would suppress their feelings for as long as possible. Why would anyone want to try to argue something that seems so unbelievable?

Society has not made it easy for transgender people to come out and, for some, they feel the only option is to live how society expects them to live. Some try for years to live their life, telling no one of the internal struggles they are facing. Too many commit suicide, and many others self-harm. Some try desperately to control their gender dysphoria by burying it deep down inside. Meanwhile, they try to do what is expected of them with regards to employment, marriage, and even children before it's finally too much for them to bear.

As young children, we are taught about the world that surrounds us from which powerful beliefs form. I would like you to reflect for a moment on what you were taught as a young child about the gospel. What beliefs were instilled in you from a young age that may be deterring you from revisiting the scriptures with an uninhibited mind? How difficult is it for you to look at that which has been ingrained in you from an early age and consider the fact that there may be more than what you have been taught? Can you consider that there may be something about your current belief that may be flawed, or that the knowledge on which your beliefs are based is incomplete?

Over the last few years, I have spoken to numerous transgender people and many confided in me that they have prayed for God to take away their gender dysphoria. Some transgender people consider themselves Christians and, like many Christians believe, God has the power to heal, to elevate suffering, and to answer prayers. They pray that their gender identity would be in alignment with the sex they were assigned at birth, yet nothing changes. Are we to believe they aren't praying hard enough or in the right way? Why do their prayers go unanswered? Is there a possibility that God thinks they are perfectly made just the way they are? Perhaps, being transgender is exactly how God intended for them to be.

CHAPTER 9

Judgment is Ugly

*"Do nothing out of selfish ambition or vain conceit.
Rather, in humility value others above yourselves."*
Philippians 2:3

There is ugliness in judgment. Too often, it is carried out by using the Bible as a tool to scorn others for that which they are being judged for. Sometimes, but not always, the one delivering the judgement is doing so with an honest desire to help steer a person towards what they deem to be a more righteous path. Sometimes, judgment is well-meaning and comes from a place of love. This is usually easy to spot, because those bringing the judgment onto another often do so softly, with an intention to support through encouragement and kindness. The question is: should those people operating from a place of sincere kindness still be judging? Is it really their place to judge?

It is noble to want to teach another something that may help foster their growth. However, what if what we are teaching is not the lessons God wants us to teach? What if we have misinterpreted the scriptures and, because of that misinterpretation, have set out to teach something that is more in keeping with our own understanding than it is with the intention of God? This is where we must take extra care, because some of the things we judge others for may not be regarded as unjust by God.

Only God should judge us, and He will. He will judge us for both the good and the bad we have done in our lives, and it is His place to do so. It is not for us to do.

In fact, we are called to be mindful of our own sins, not the sins of another. (And, let me be clear, I am not suggesting that being transgender is a sin, because I do not believe it is.) Yet, we often find reserving judgement difficult to do. We are drawn to point out the shortcomings of our neighbours and compelled to speak condemnation over one another. What's worse is some deliver condemnation in bold and unnecessarily hurtful ways, with little or no regard for the harm they are causing to another through such actions. A difference of opinion is okay and often anticipated, especially around topics as controversial as this. However, we should not use these differences to bear ill will towards one another.

A person who is experiencing gender dysphoria and

finds themselves on a transgender path is particularly vulnerable. Some transgender people are already suffering and often tormented within themselves as they try to make sense out of the disconnect they are feeling between their mind and their body. They don't need to be further plagued by people who feel right in judging them or be subjected to counsel that tells them that denying their transgender identity is the only way to be saved.

We all want acceptance and approval from a young age. We want our parents, friends and teachers to accept and approve of us as small children. Later, we seek the approval and acceptance of our spouse or partner, friends, associates, and bosses. Think how much more difficult this must be for a transgender person. By their very nature, they are different – judged and treated as lesser by society. How much harder it must be for them to gain acceptance and approval. They are often turned away from their church communities, their friends, places of employment, and even their own families – all for just being who they are.

I wish I had a magic wand that would put an immediate end to the disapproval, discrimination, and stigma that transgender people endure on a regular basis.

We can never truly understand or know the

difficulties of another unless we have walked in their shoes. Colossians 3:12 instructs us to be compassionate towards one another: "Therefore, as God's chosen people, holy and dearly loved, clothe yourselves with compassion, kindness, humility, gentleness and patience." This is in alignment with our calling to love one another as ourselves.

So, why do so many people feel a need to not only judge one another, but do so without kindness, without humility, gentleness, or patience? How about those that protest, shouting demeaning slurs and holding up signs plastered with hateful words and detestable messages that degrade and dehumanize the transgender community? To provide you with only a small taste of the judgment transgender people face every day, the following are just a few examples of things too often said to them:

"You are vile and disgusting."

"You don't deserve to live."

"The world would be better off if you killed yourself."

"You are an abomination."

"You are a disgraceful excuse for a human being."

"The devil lives inside you."

"You are sick."

"You are mentally ill."

And, one we have already proven scientifically to be incorrect: "There are only two sexes."

The point is that being the subject of so much hate and condemnation is hard, exhausting, and downright devastating. This is why so many transgender people look to suicide as a way out. They may not have always had a desire to die, but through the brutal and negative treatment others have doled out towards them, their strength may have weakened. It is not difficult to understand how some transgender people would believe they may never be accepted.

In a world where empathy and grace seem lacking and intolerance and even hate appear to run rampant, it can seem as if we are getting farther away from God, rather than closer to Him.

Those that are vulnerable see hate and judgement all around them. It weighs on them until, one day, they no longer have it in them to fight. People, through their words and actions, have driven some in this vulnerable group to take their own lives. Some of the people that say hurtful things say they are not responsible for the high suicide rates among transgender people. They believe that they are not guilty, that they didn't point the gun or pull the trigger.

They are, however, an accessory and a very willing, active participant. They could have chosen grace, shown compassion and love, but instead, they chose hate and intolerance. They believed, for whatever reason, that their approach was valid, or perhaps, cited free speech as another excuse to act with such contempt. Don't get me wrong, I do believe in free speech. I just think we can use our voice to bring up valid points without damaging the fabric of another human being in the process.

No matter how they justify spewing hatred towards another, it goes against everything the Bible calls on us to do and to be. In 1 John 2:9-17, it says:

> Anyone who claims to be in the light but hates a brother or sister is still in the darkness. Anyone who loves their brother and sister lives in the light, and there is nothing in them to make them stumble. But anyone who hates a brother or sister is in the darkness and walks around in the darkness. They do not know where they are going, because the darkness has blinded them.

Using the Bible as a tool to bring pain and suffering to another person is never the right thing to do. Cherry-picking passages to use against people is unfortunately far too commonplace today. My response to that is quite simple: if we are to believe one passage is true, then we must believe them all to be true. If we are going to use scripture, we should be consistent in our use of it. We should not use those passages where we have nothing to lose so easily against another, and then decide those where we do have something to lose should be absolute.

We cannot look at Deuteronomy 22:5 in the Old Testament, where it states, "A woman must not wear men's clothing, nor a man wear women's clothing, for the LORD your God detests anyone who does this," nor Leviticus 18:22, also in the Old Testament, where it says, "Do not have sexual relations with a man as one does with a woman; that is detestable," and demand that society respect and honour these passages if we are not prepared to give equal weight to all other passages in the Old Testament. There are hundreds of laws found in the Old Testament.

However, there are only a few that people pull out and say others should abide by, while at the same time, saying it is acceptable to ignore dozens, if not hundreds, more.

How about Exodus 21:7? "If a man sells his daughter as a servant, she is not to go free as male servants do." How many of the people that use Leviticus 18:22 against the LGBTQ community believe it is okay to not only sell their daughters into slavery, but to do so without allowing them to be freed after six years, the way the male slaves were?

How about in the books of Mark and Matthew, where we are told that children that rebel against their parents are to be put to death? I think we can all agree that most teenagers rebel against their parents at one time or another. If we were putting children to death for parental rebellion, few children would ever make it to adulthood. Thank goodness that is not a cherry-picked passage we are expected to uphold!

There are passages we dismiss today as being irrelevant because adhering to them does not serve us in modern times. We give consideration to the culture in which we live. Most Christians also recognize the reason we disregard much of the Old Testament, like the laws in Leviticus, is because we have come under the new laws of Christ. Through the Resurrection, the laws of the Old Testament are fulfilled and no longer attributable to our lives.

The new laws of the New Testament took over as the new covenant between God and humanity. If we are going to follow the new law, perhaps the one we should take note of is the one in Matthew 7:12, where it states, "So in everything, do to others what you would have them do to you, for this sums up the Law and the Prophets."

Both the Old and New Testaments are still considered sacred scriptures. The Old Testament established the foundations and principles around Christianity, while the New Testament provides the new rules through which Christ's followers fashion their lives. The Bible commands us to "Love the Lord your God with all your heart and all your soul" and to "love thy neighbour as yourself." If we can also extend respect and compassion to others without judgement, we can honour God and live the life Jesus would want us to live all at the same time.

CHAPTER 10

Trying to Understand

"Be completely humble and gentle; be patient,
bearing with one another in love."
Ephesians 4:2

Unless you are the parent of a transgender child and have walked a mile in our shoes, it is almost impossible to understand the full extent of our experience. Parenting is important work, but no one claims it is easy. Mix in having a transgender child, and parents find themselves swimming in a whole new set of challenges. On top of that, we quickly discover society doesn't appear to be on our side. Others will disagree with our parenting style and make no bones about sharing their unsolicited and unwelcome opinions with us. Many will persist in their insistence that our child's non-binary identity of self is not real.

There is discrimination all around, and it is not only directed towards our children, but often, towards us as parents – suggesting we are to blame. While some people are downright cruel to transgender children, many recognize they are children and so turn their insults and snarky comments towards the parents and families. Some have even suggested we have, somehow, allowed this, nurtured this, and even encouraged our children to be transgender. Some call us unfit and suggest our children should be removed from our care.

Let me assure you that no parent would ever choose this for their child. It is a difficult path to walk, and difficult is never what we want for our children. Most of us – at least initially – are scared to death of what might lie ahead for our transgender child. This is partly why so many of us refer to our children as brave. They will often exhibit a determination and courage beyond anything we can mobilize.

Being the parent of a transgender child is often a lonely road, where you feel as if you have far more enemies than friends around you. Even the most supportive of friends rarely understands the journey you and your family are on, no matter how much you share with them.

Having said that, we do need our friends. There is a peace that we feel as parents when we are in the presence of true friends that allows us to drop our guard and breathe easier, knowing they are there. Sometimes, we act in unexpected ways, clamming up with those closest to us because, frankly, we may be exhausted. We may be depleted from having to face mean and unscrupulous people. Other times, we may need to vent, to talk it out, as we desperately just want to be heard. We may even reach a point where we just need to explode – or even implode – into an emotional wreck for a minute or two. When this happens, we are incredibly grateful for our friends and for their unconditional, non-judgmental support.

I would love to give you a clear picture of some of what we are dealing with as parents of transgender children, because then, it might be easier to understand our experiences. A fellow parent, Koreen Pagano, put together a terrific list of the many things we are faced with when our teenage children come out to us as transgender. This list was originally published on her *Learning in Tandem* blog, and Koreen has graciously provided me with permission to share this list with you here:

- Learn what the term transgender means (most cis folks don't learn about this until circumstances prompt our education, unfortunately)
- Learn what the transgender experience is like
- Advocate with school staff, healthcare professionals, extracurricular event instructors
- Be supportive of the challenges your kiddo is

    facing

- Use new pronouns
- Use a new name for your child that you likely didn't choose
- Navigate the opinions of everyone you meet
- Navigate the opinions of your family and friends
- Navigate the emotional response of your partner, if you have one
- Navigate your own sense of loss, grief for the dreams you had formed for your child, for who you had believed that they were or who they were becoming
- Navigate and develop new dreams and expectations of who your child really is
- Face the realities of how your trans kiddo may be treated in the world
- Try to navigate your deepest fears of violence against your child
- Try to navigate your deepest fears of violence your child might commit against themselves
- Come to terms with statistics
- Learn about blockers, hormones and trans healthcare. Understand and weigh the pros and cons.
- Realize how big of a deal bathrooms are for

trans folks. Understand why.

If I were to add a point to this list, it would be to learn when to respond and when to ignore the derogatory comments hurled at us by others, including other parents. It's more difficult than I imagined remaining silent, though I know that is likely the best way to handle many of the comments directed at us.

As a mother whose instinct is to protect her children, my mama bear claws come out from time to time. I want to strike back, but instead – more often than not – I will take a deep breath in and try to calm myself. Wisdom has taught me that there are people who are not ready to listen; people who have already made up their minds about us before they even hear the details of our story; people who don't want to know our journey; and people who don't accept that what we might be doing in supporting and helping our children transition may actually be what is best for them.

Perhaps, it is safe to assume that unless you are parenting a transgender child, you have never given thought to these types of things. Many of the challenges we must face as the parent of a transgender child likely sound foreign to you. For many of us, the points on Koreen's list were initially foreign to us, as well. It wasn't until we were faced with the situation of having a transgender child that many of us even thought to become educated. It is the sad truth. Most people don't take the time to educate themselves on a subject until they are directly affected by it.

Your decision to read this book tells me you are different. You are obviously looking to expand your knowledge, and that is always a positive thing. Even though you may disagree with some, perhaps even all, of what I'm writing about, you have opened yourself up to reading more about it. I applaud you for that.

I wish I was more proactive in my education of LGBTQ people before my son came out to me, but that is water under the bridge now. I hope that by sharing our story in *I Promised Not to Tell,* I have made up for some of my ignorance by helping others along their own path to a clearer understanding.

Some of us parents cope better than others, as do our children. Some of our children are out to the world and others choose to live a stealth life, which means only those closest to them know they are transgender. The latter is how my son, Jordan, is currently living his own life.

Along this journey, the saddest part for some of us is when we learn that some of the people closest to us are against us. Some of us are even forced to choose between our children and our partners, parents, and other family members. For example, you would like to believe that your children's grandparents will stick by them, and stick by their own children who are parenting their transgender grandchild, but that is not always the case. The decision(s) to separate or remove certain people from our lives doesn't just affect us and our transgender child, but our other children and extended family, as well. Of course, when presented with such a choice, we chose our children, but that doesn't make severing ties any easier. Extended family members can cause us great heartache and pain. Conversely, when they are loving and accepting, as my own parents were, it makes our world so much brighter.

If there was a greater understanding and wider acceptance of transgender children, fewer families would find themselves in these difficult positions. Therefore, we must keep the conversation going. We must continue to share our stories so that we can continue to humanize transgender people. When all is said and done, transgender people may live with an unusual set of challenges, but they also have far more in common than not with cisgender people.

Being transgender is just one facet of their being, and many transgender people just wish to go about their day-to-day lives without the stigma that comes from others knowing their gender history. Transgender people are just people who, like everyone else, have the right to be recognized as individuals without others putting unnecessary emphasis on their gender.

Ultimately, I don't think others can fully understand any more than we, as cisgender parents, can fully understand the individual transgender journey our own children are on. Even though our children may shake their heads at us and tell us that we don't understand them, they will also forgive us for our shortcomings. This is because they see that we are trying and because they know, above all else, that we love them. I just wish that alone was enough.

As I am putting the final touches on this chapter, I am once again shaken by the reality our children face. In a private Facebook group for parents of transgender children, a mother shares with us the news that her child's life has come to an abrupt end. It is unnatural that a child predeceases a parent. It is our worse fear coming true.

A beautiful soul, lovingly called Finn, is now gone. His broken-hearted mother, who must be in unimaginable pain, asks all of us to keep sharing, keep talking, encouraging us to elevate the conversation about Finn and all our beautiful transgender children. She understands her loss is felt deeply throughout the group. Many of us – even those that had never met Finn – express our condolences to her and her family while shedding our own tears of deep sorrow. We hug our children just a little tighter, reminded again of the harsh reality which too many of us have come to know.

To those of you that are trying to understand us and our transgender children, thank you.

CHAPTER 11

In Humility, There is Truth

"Finally, all of you, be like-minded, be sympathetic, love one another, be compassionate and humble."
1 Peter 3:8

The reality is that we just don't know what we don't know. As we have learned, there is some proof in science that there is an area of the brain where our gender identity stems from. Scientific evidence resulting from studies of the brain and the brains of deceased transgender individuals offer us some information on how gender dysphoria can form. These findings can offer some peace to those who seek a biological explanation. It is possible, in time, that science will be able to tell us far more than it can today about transgender people and the root cause of gender dysphoria. I, for one, look forward to that day, and not because I require information for myself, but so that information is available to those that need it – those that need further confirmation to accept and understand transgender people are not choosing to be transgender. Being transgender is not a cultural thing, a trend, or something that has been nurtured into people through parenting, social conditioning, or society.

If we were being honest about how difficult life can be for transgender people, we would know that no one would purposely seek to be transgender. There is nothing simple or easy about the life path of a transgender person. Much of what they need to go through to be truly happy can be daunting, exhausting, and in some cases, downright painful. Being transgender is not a choice, but choosing to transition is, and that is something no one would ever choose to go through unless they felt it was necessary. Yet, rather than help support transgender youth, many families use scripture as an excuse to exhibit the most un-Christ-like behaviour towards their children, including tossing them out onto the street.

Faith is not science, yet those of us that have a strong faith understand the level of conviction a person can have for something, even something we cannot see or prove. I have an unwavering faith in God and His intentional desire to build us this wonderful diverse world in which we live. My faith tells me that transgender people are a deliberate creation of God and that to do anything short of loving them would be to denounce God and deny His creation. I feel that to use biblical text as a tool to say something is absolutely certain is a bit arrogant. Sure, we can have our own interpretations, but to be egotistical and say we know God's intentions is something I am not prepared to do.

Whatever opinions we hold, faith is something no one can prove without a shadow of a doubt. To use our interpretations or beliefs as a tool against people is not only unfair, it's pretentious. We weren't there when the Bible was written, nor did we speak to or have personal contact with any of the people depicted in the Bible. We must realize that our own biases filter into our individual interpretations in the same way the contributing biblical storytellers' biases would have filtered into their stories. Even those of us that believe in the text can't say with absolute certainty that the Bible is completely non-fiction – perhaps, there is fiction woven in.

I can feel the anger in some of you right now – how dare I suggest the Bible is fiction? I understand how that would be upsetting to some, but please allow me to offer you a different perspective, as an author. I am not a fiction author. However, I do have great respect for those writers who are. As a non-fiction writer, I already know the people in my stories, so I can describe them and present them to the reader in an authentic way.

Conversely, to write a fiction book, an author must imagine and create each character in such a way that they are interesting, intriguing, and compelling enough to draw the reader in. For those who have a protagonist and secondary characters that are well developed, an author can even draw readers through multiple books in a series, which takes great talent. In addition to character development, an excellent fiction writer must be a good researcher. They must research real places and times so that when they write stories that take place in certain areas, their books are believable. Historic events and places must be accurately depicted with the highest degree of accuracy. The more specific and detailed the fiction author can describe the setting and scenes, the more credible the author's stories will be.

I have heard people say they know the Bible is non-fiction because what it foretells has come to pass for them. They have lived the experience that the Bible promises. For example, the Bible says if you confess your sins to God, you will be forgiven and relieved of the burden of your guilt. Some claim this is exactly what they have done. They have confessed, and following their confession, a great weight was lifted and they emerged unburdened. Living through this experience only serves to further strengthen their faith because the promised result is experienced by them just as the scriptures revealed it would be.

However, do we really know that their experience was based on reality, or is that which they believe so deeply believed that they create their own experience? Faith is a powerful thing and those that have it understand it is not easily shaken. The intangibles of faith make it impossible to prove whether we are the ones creating our own destiny, or if God really is intervening. Perhaps, the act of believing in something with such conviction can make it come to pass.

The Bible has foretold things that science later proved were true. For example, a strange passage in Hebrews 11:3 reads: "By faith we understand that the universe was formed at God's command, so that what is seen was not made out of what was visible." Today, we understand all things we view with our eyes are made up of many things that are invisible to us. The protons, neutrons, and electrons which are at the base of all atoms are not visible to us, yet grade nine science class taught us they exist. We understand the energy of all things, while not tangible or visible, does exist. This is not the only example out there. If you look, you will find several that appear to validate the Bible as an accurate and believable book.

Considering what I have described in the paragraphs above, we need to admit that, however unlikely, it is possible that the Bible could be an exquisitely thought out and well-crafted book of fiction. The Bible could be a book so well-written by the original writer(s), who understood that the story would need to be detailed, using historical evidence of actual places and people to become a book that would stand the test of time. This book would become recognized as a book of non-fiction, when in fact, it may be a skillful creation of pure fiction.

I am not saying the Bible is fiction, nor suggesting that this is what I personally believe to be true. I am only suggesting that, if it is fiction, it would make complete sense that so many of the places described within its text are accurately described. The fact that a book, any book, contains stories of real places and real people doesn't mean the stories are, in fact, true. It won't be until we leave this plane and come face to face with our God that we will have the answer.

While the Bible provides a reason to have a moral compass, do we want that to be the only reason we have one? Shouldn't we all live just and moral lives regardless of whether we believe the Bible to be true or not? Shouldn't we all have a moral compass that points us towards loving our neighbours because it's the right thing to do, and not because we fear the mighty wrath of God if we don't? Shouldn't we strive to live by a moral code that treats everyone with dignity, respect, and honour and do so not out of fear, but out of love? Let's be fully present in the life we have now so we can appreciate it and respect it as the gift that it is. Let's not use our time here to force our views onto one another, but rather, appreciate that our greatest lessons may come from those that are different from us. We should not be threatened or fearful of people with divergent views. We should instead seek to further conversations with them, to become more educated about things we may have little understanding of, like the transgender community.

What if God is real and the Bible is a non-fiction book, as so many believe? What if the biggest test of all is to place us among such a diverse society to see if we can truly be non-judgmental and love our neighbours without discrimination? What if transgender people are intentionally created and their journey is to help us all to be more compassionate, tolerant, accepting, and honouring toward all of God's creations? Just like in the animal and plant kingdoms, where there are more than two genders, is it so impossible to comprehend that the same could not be true among the human population? We who are proud and arrogant and full of ego believe we have all the answers, but what if we can just pause long enough to consider that we just don't know what we don't know?

Upon reflection, I have thought about the talents God gives out to people – the natural talent that He bestows on His children. Some say God is against LGBTQ people. If that were true, I often wonder how there are so many LGBTQ people with incredible God-given talent. Take Elton John, for example; anyone who is familiar with his music would have to agree that he has a huge gift. Elton is an openly gay man who has been with his now husband for decades. In 2014, after same sex marriage became legal in England, he and his partner were married. Together, the couple has two sons. If God somehow felt their union was a sin, don't you think Elton's success would have been blocked in some way? The exact opposite is true, and his career has soared. Elton is now more than seventy years young and still entertaining people around the globe with his incredible talent.

Jodie Foster, Lily Tomlin, and Ellen DeGeneres are other LGBTQ people who seem blessed and supported by God. Their talent, careers, and success is grand. Ellen has certainly been blessed with a venue from which to speak and influence the world. This is just a tiny sample of the people who have been super blessed with not only talent, but great success. It certainly seems as if God's blessings have fallen on their lives.

At the same time, you see good, honest, God-loving, cisgender, heterosexual people working hard who never seem to catch a break. It's as if God just isn't showing up for them. I realize this is an oversimplification, but my point is that God is alive and working within the lives of LGBTQ people in a way that supports the notion that He is not an anti-LGBTQ God.

I mentioned in my first book (*I Promised Not to Tell*) that one minister had prepared a Bible study around the idea that Jesus will not return until the churches invite everyone in – until the time that all churches become welcoming, inclusive places for everyone, including LGBTQ people. He puts forth a rather convincing argument. What if that minister is correct? What if the anti-LGBTQ teachings put forth by some churches are actively keeping the saviour away? Many believe the exact opposite; they believe that LGBTQ people are corrupting society and their very behaviour is what is keeping Jesus from returning. I have provided a link to the study I'm making mention to in the resource section at the back of this book, should you wish to review it.

It is so amazing, but at the same time, perplexing how two people can read the exact same biblical texts and interpret them so completely differently. Our vastly different views have created quite a predicament within many of our homes and our churches. Perhaps, we see the interpretation we need to see or the one that will best serve our needs. Maybe, as our position in life changes, so will our interpretations.

It is far easier to be a follower than a leader, and therefore, easier to just go along with whatever the current teachings of the Bible are today. It is bold, brave, and very scary to step out and offer an interpretation that goes against what we have always believed to be true. This doesn't mean we shouldn't do it. We should always challenge how we are interpreting scriptures, especially when something about the current teachings seems off.

Today, teaching against the LGBTQ community seems off to me. We are not giving any weight to the new discoveries we have made around sexuality and gender. It feels as if we are ignoring that the world we live in today is vastly different than the one that existed when the scriptures were written. I cannot help but think that so many families could be saved from being torn apart if only we would consider that maybe, just maybe, some of us are standing on the wrong side of history.

Those of us that are passionate about our opinions

of the Bible would love to have the support and agreement of others. It's natural to want to have your interpretation understood and embraced, but it's not easy to sway people, especially around things as controversial as gender. If you've come this far in the book, I thank you for sticking with me. I hope that if we disagree on what the Bible says about transgender people, we can at least agree to disagree respectfully. The one thing I know for certain is that arguing with one another over interpretation is not the answer.

Jesus warns us in the scriptures of religious self-righteousness, and I believe that there is a way to carry out these conversations while remaining respectful of one another. Usually, people who are so completely fixed in their interpretations aren't open to hearing any other interpretation, and this seems a bit sad and short-sighted. Then, there are those that are more open – people who are willing to listen to another's opinion and even give fair weight to it. When we can have respectful conversations in this way over the scriptures, we all win.

I really enjoy speaking with different people about their faith, especially when it differs from my own. I find it rather fascinating to learn about their beliefs, religious customs, and practices. We can see things from different perspectives and we may even be surprised at how those different perspectives resonate with us. Then again, maybe all they will serve to do is cement our own thoughts on the scriptures. This is also valid, as it reinforces our faith as being just that – ours. It assures us that we have true faith, which is not easily shaken.

We should appreciate one another as the individual thinkers that we are. We should also refrain from bashing others for their interpretations in hurtful ways because, as I have said before, we just don't know what we don't know. Wisdom is a trait we should all strive for and one that is rarely reached through belittling or disrespecting others.

As we approach the end of this book, you may feel as if you have more questions than answers. Perhaps, that is the way God intended it – that we would seek more than we would find; that we would make this life a great quest and a learning experience that would have us expand and grow as spiritual beings. The Bible is a wonderful tool, but like any tool, it is up to us to decide how to use it.

Love should not be lost when we traverse between the biblical world and the world as it is today. Let's try to always be compassionate and remember to extend grace to one another, because we never know the journey that another person is on. We are all growing and evolving as we weave our way through this wonderful thing called life.

What about those people who continue to insist that transgender people are living a life that is against God? To answer that question, we should look to John 10:10, where we are instructed by our Lord on how to discern between Him and Satan. It states: "The thief comes only to steal and kill and destroy; I have come that they may have life and have it to the fill."

For Satan to wreak havoc in our lives, what better way than to strike at the heart of our families and our relationships? To move families to toss out their children, pit spouses and partners against one another, and even cause people to leave or be tossed from their faith communities. Does this sound like the actions God would want people to take?

God has instructed us to love, to accept one another, and to not be divided. Satan, on the other hand, is revelling in the glory we are bestowing on him when we continue to put hate, shame, and fear above unconditional love and acceptance. Satan is about creating chaos, uncertainty, and doubt, but God is about none of these things. God instills confidence, strength, serenity, and above all, love.

If you still are having difficulty accepting that transgender people are an intentional creation of God, I challenge you to leave any judgment to Him. Expressing love and kindness to all of humanity is to live as Jesus himself lived. Jesus did not forsake anyone, nor did he turn his back on others. If Jesus were a parent, he would not have turned away from a transgender child and he certainly would not have tossed them from his life. Focus only on loving and accepting the transgender people whose paths cross yours. In doing so, know that you are doing as God has asked you to do. In the end, we must remember we are called to love.

John 15:12 says, "This is my commandment that you love one another as I have loved you." We should remember 1 Corinthians 13:4: "Love is patient, love is kind," and 1 Corinthians 13:7: "It always protects, always trusts, always hopes, always perseveres." Finally, let us not forget 1 Corinthians 16:14: "Let all that you do be done with love."

Is it not more peaceful to live in a world where we invite everyone to the assembly? Where everyone is welcome to the table? To choose that kind of world *is* to choose God.

CHAPTER 12 - BONUS CHAPTER

What Does God Think?

As promised in the introduction, I am including this chapter as a bonus for you. This is a chapter from my earlier published memoir, I Promised Not to Tell: Raising a transgender child. I hope you enjoy it and that it offers you a bit more of our family's story.

Even though in my heart I knew that Jordan was, in fact, a transgender male, I could not help but wonder: what does God think?

I consider myself a spiritual person and I do believe in God. If ever there was a time in my life where I needed some divine reassurance, it was then. At the time, I had been working with a life coach, a strong woman of God, whom I felt compelled to turn to for advice. Her advice was to refer me to a trusted family friend and counsellor that she had used to work through some issues in her own life. The funny thing is I had heard this coach say, on numerous occasions, "Look to Me, Not to Man" as advice to always turn to God first for answers.

On this day, however, she didn't turn me to God. She turned me to man. Actually, *woman* would be more accurate, as it was a female counsellor she recommended I contact. I went ahead and called the counsellor my coach had referred me to, and almost immediately, got a weird feeling that this was a mistake. Intuition is a crazy thing and I am learning to trust mine more and more as the years go on.

The conversation went on for over an hour, with me doing very little talking. I explained that we believed our daughter, Jordan, was actually a transgender male and we were about to embark on the journey of helping him transition to his true self. The initial response was that she was glad I had called and that she could definitely help me, and help Jordan to love her female self.

She proceeded to refer me to scripture after scripture in the Bible. It is amazing that I was able to write them all down because I was crying so hard. I did manage to share the story of Mariah confiding in a couple who told her that being transgender was "not of God." She said I should not worry, that we could "fix" Jordan.

The decision to "fix" Jordan was almost an automatic response. It was not a conclusion that was arrived at after a long look into Jordan, Jordan's history, or even Jordan's current state of mind. Heck, this person had never even laid eyes on Jordan, and I certainly wasn't being given an opportunity to provide much information during the call. I could hardly get a word in the entire time. It was obvious to me that the circumstances didn't matter. It was a case of her mind already being made up that there was no such thing as a transgender person and this child just needed to be fixed. She wanted to schedule another call at the end, but I declined, saying I'd have to get back to her on that. Of course, I never did.

After the call ended, I just sat alone in my bedroom and wept like a baby. Then, I prayed. I prayed in the morning and I prayed in the evening. I have never prayed so hard. "Please, God, help me understand. Help us make the right decisions for Jordan. Help us do the right thing."

When I prayed, I heard the same message again and again: "Help Your Son." "Help Your Son." Of course, God would surely know Jordan better than anyone else, and certainly better than some counsellor who barely asked me anything about Jordan's childhood, our family, or our life. I continued to pray and God continued to deliver me only one message: "Help Your Son." Okay! I hear you.

The Bible is an interesting book that is used by so many to prove a point this way or that way. I did something few people actually do. I set out to read it for myself, word for word, paragraph by paragraph, page by page, chapter by chapter. Perhaps, saying book by book would be more accurate than chapter by chapter when discussing the Bible. Regardless, I expect you get my point, which is that I approached it the same way I approach any other book.

My reading included both the Old and New Testaments. It took me seven months to complete it. Even though I felt a sense of accomplishment when I was finished, I recognized that having read the Bible in no way made me an expert on it. I am not prepared to try to formally debunk religious theory or confirm it. However, I did make some interesting observations while reading it.

In my opinion, there appears to be many inconsistencies within the Bible. Biblical text is difficult for a layman like me to decipher. To thoroughly understand it, you have to not just read the words in the sentences, but look at the context of those sentences. You need to be aware of the smallest nuances and even give consideration to the person speaking. You must determine if the person speaking is testifying to their own account of events, or if they are quoting someone else. My point is that most people, if they study it long enough, can interpret any passage or combination of passages in such a way that it either supports their case or refutes someone else's.

For anyone who struggles with the Bible and believes that being transgender is against God, I found something that may be of interest. What I found was some interesting biblical teachings on eunuchs and eunuch prophecies. It is an in-depth Bible study, including flow charts, prepared by Brian Bowen Ministries and it can be found at www.eunuchflow. blogspot.ca. The main idea presented is that Jesus wants the churches to be all inclusive by inviting everyone in. The study suggests that until all people, including LGBT people, are treated the same as everyone else by the church, Jesus will not return.

The word of God says, "love thy neighbour." It doesn't say, "love thy neighbour except for the ones you do not like." There are non-gender conforming people in the Bible and God doesn't strike any of them dead, nor does Jesus turn away from them. It also says in the Bible that God looks at one's heart, not at one's outward appearance. I am not sure if you see gender when you think of God, but I don't. For me, when it says we were created in God's image, it's about having a heart and spirit like God. It is not about one's outer image or specific gender.

There are things in the Bible I disagree with,

conditions or practices that may have made sense back in biblical times, but today, would be met with widespread disapproval. For example, men having multiple wives and fathering children from their multiple wives. How about girls marrying and giving birth when they are still small children? That is all acceptable in the Bible.

Here's a thought: if God didn't mean for girls to have babies at twelve and thirteen years of age, why did he make it so they could? In biblical times, I believe it was necessary to populate for survival. To put it simply, there is strength in numbers. This was needed at the time to grow and defend one's territory. Under these circumstances, it made sense for one man to father multiple children with multiple wives. The reality is we do not live in biblical times.

Today, we enjoy benefits like modern medicine. Heart bypass surgery and pacemakers are two examples of how we can alter the outcome of one's life that were not available in biblical times. Does that mean just because modern medicine wasn't available back then, that we shouldn't use it today? Some religions dictate exactly that. To live a modern-day life on the literal teachings of the Bible, to me, seems ludicrous.

I choose to live a life based on love and compassion towards my fellow human beings. If someone believes

I'm doing a disservice to God in some way by doing that, well, that's their issue, not mine. Having said that, I also think it is worthy to note that I do have respect for others that have a different opinion and choose to follow a different path. I absolutely respect a person's right to have their own opinions, no matter how much I may disagree with those opinions. I believe that respecting another's rights to interpret the Bible and draw their own conclusion about what God wants for them is important. Provided of course, their own interpretations are not used as punishment against others. Using the Bible as a tool to manipulate, judge, or condemn others seems to be little about love and more about hate. I do not believe God intended that to be the message.

I hope that this conveys to you that I am not out to challenge your religion or to have you turn away from that which you believe. I understand that religion plays a very important role, and for some, it can be at the very root of their soul. While not all religious people feel conflict, I bring it up because it saddens me deeply when I see the torment some families go through when they struggle with transgenderism and religion.

Why is it so easy to accept that people can be born with something extra, missing, or mismatched, like a limb, but can't have something extra, missing, or mismatched with their brain? Obviously, we can't "see" the brain, but we can clearly see where a limb is, or isn't meant to be. Seriously, though, just because we can't see something doesn't mean we should just assume it is as we expect it to be. Is it impossible to believe that there could be something in the brain that doesn't align with the person's exterior?

I feel thankful that my beliefs allow me to accept that transgender people are not against God, but I understand that not everyone shares my beliefs. What helps me to see transgender people as sharing an equal place among God's children is that I believe they were born that way. I also believe that love is the most important emotion of all. I have read many near death experience stories, and there seems to be a common thread among them; that thread is love.

Religion, while it has its purpose and offers great comfort to many, it also has its weaknesses. I see rigidness in many religions that can block love and leave the door open for shame, fear, and even hate. In addition to my belief in God, I also believe that we are all spiritual beings having a human experience. When I think of what a spiritual being is, I do not see gender. Gender, to me, only comes into play in our human experience, and because I believe this, accepting people of all genders, even genders that differ from their assigned sex at birth, is easy. I'm fortunate to believe what I do, as it certainly makes it easier for me to be there for my child without fear of God or fear of judgement of others.

If someone's beliefs make acceptance difficult for them, I hope they can find peace and love before permanent damage is done to their relationships. Perhaps, seeking guidance from their own spiritual counsellor may help. Accepting something and agreeing with it is not the same thing. Through love and compassion, there is a way to accept things, even things we do not fully understand. A way to hopefully protect the relationship you have with any transgender person(s) in your life. I hope that would be your end goal, to find a way to protect your relationship and be able to continue to love that person, regardless of your beliefs. God acknowledges each person has free will, so to live peacefully we need to find a way to accept others as they are.

It may help to remember that no one lives their life according to the Bible. They can only live their life according to their interpretation of the Bible. There's a big difference. We should embrace the fact that we are individual thinkers. We should question, study, and learn for ourselves, rather than blindly follow the interpretation of another. We all have different paths to follow, different purposes to fulfill, and we cannot successfully do that if we do not exercise our own abilities to hear God's word for ourselves. Listen to the word for yourself, filter out the noise of others, and draw on your own strength to interpret it for yourself.

I believe God loves ALL His children, and by ALL, I mean exactly that. My belief allows me to follow His direction, "Help Your Son," without question. I turned to God and not to man. I got guidance and I chose to follow it. I no longer search for approval from others. My conscience is clear.

Some of my Christian friends who are unaware of my son's history openly share their anti-LGBT thoughts with me. It is difficult for me, trying to express my own thoughts and positions on the issues without being so passionate as to arouse suspicion about where my motivation is coming from. That may sound like I don't care about other members of the LGBT community, only my son. That's not true. However, when you are so close to a situation, there is a motivation that emanates from that, driving you to speak out; at least, that's how it is for me, personally.

Many of my friends have children and grandchildren of their own. I wonder if their own children or grandchildren were transgender, how they would handle it. Would they take them for therapy to "fix" them? Would they inquire about shock treatments and other invasive therapies that once were accepted but now discarded? How far down the path would they go before they reached acceptance? If it were their children or grandchildren that didn't fit into our binary definitions of male and female, would they put love first and rally together? These are good people, honest, caring people I am talking about. I want to believe their anti-LGBT, specifically anti-transgender positions would quickly crumble if they were talking about someone they love, but I honestly don't know if it would.

Jim and I believe in the church of family. Given the choice of loving and supporting a family member or adhering to the teachings of a church or religion, it is no contest. The family member and their well-being will always be our priority. Sometimes, the best way we can serve God is by honouring and taking care of that which has already been given to us. This, in my case, is my children. Today, Jordan is healthy and strong. We love and accept him for exactly who he is, our son.

If you are a parent of a transgender child, especially if you are struggling with that reality, know that you are not alone. Whether you believe in God or not, believe in yourself. Believe that there is no one that knows your child the way you do. Believe that you are well-equipped to love your child. At the root of it all, there must be love. You loved your child when they were born and you have loved them up to this point. Please, continue to love them now and after they transition. Ignore the criticisms of others; they will criticize you regardless.

We should be grateful our children are alive to love. We should be thankful we can continue to share our lives with them, regardless of whether they are male or female. It is a heart-wrenching time, for some more so than for others, but if you make it about love, not gender, you will get through this journey; that, I can promise you.

Thank You

I want to thank you for picking up this book and coming along on this journey of discovery with me. I understand that my writing is not that of a highly accredited academic scholar and that it lacks a certain level of sophistication, but that was the point. As a layperson, I set out to present this writing to you in as straightforward a manner as possible, giving you a layman's view. I hope it connects with readers who, like me, are not scholars, theologians, or neuroscientists, but rather, just regular people who desire more information on this exceedingly controversial topic. I wanted to ignite curiosity and have us consider some things we may not have considered before. I wanted to open a dialogue that everyone could feel a part of, and I hope I have achieved that for you.

I hope that you have enjoyed this writing and found it worthy of your time and attention. If this book has served in some way to lessen the burden about what God thinks and the Bible says about transgender people, I am thankful. If you are a transgender person or have a loved one who is, I hope you believe without a doubt that transgender people are wonderfully and purposely made. Nothing should hold any of us down for being the unique being that God created us to be.

Perhaps, you have been struggling to understand how a transgender person can not only be Christian, but fit in with the beliefs of Christianity. Or perhaps, you were just curious about the topic and wanted an opportunity to explore it further. Either way, I thank you.

This is undoubtedly a polarizing debate with deeply held beliefs on both sides. While I understand this book may have done little to change societal perspectives, I do hope it has, at the very least, served to soften the divide that exists among some Christians.

I would like to encourage you to tell others about this book so we can continue to unite all of God's children by helping to bridge the gap between conservative Evangelical Christians and the more progressive Christians among us.

As always, I invite my readers to connect with me through a private email address I have set up for just that purpose. That email address is: writtenbymom@gmail.com. I promise to make a conscious effort to respond to your emails as quickly as possible.

I would like to end by quoting Luna Adriana: "God gave us eyes to see the beauty in nature and hearts to see the beauty in each other."

Sincerely,

Cheryl B. Evans

P.S. If you enjoyed this book, please take a few moments and give it a positive review. Positive reviews will encourage more people to read it. That way, together, we can help educate others on this topic and on how we can greatly improve our culture for everyone through compassion, understanding, and love. If we are fortunate, perhaps, we will soften the hearts and minds of those that have, until this point, believed that being transgender is against God and the Bible.

Book Club Talking Points

What Does God Think? by Cheryl B. Evans.

This controversial book can be a real conversation starter for book clubs everywhere. Here are some suggested questions club members may want to ponder after reading *What Does God Think?*

1. How did the author make you feel about your own position on this polarizing topic?

2. What surprising new things did you discover about transgender people you didn't know?

3. Was there a particular scripture that spoke to you? If so, which one?

4. Was there a point in the book that you strongly disagreed with? What part?

5. Do you feel it was fair for the author to compare past religious indiscretions with how we are treating the transgender community today? Why or Why not?

6. Did you find the scientific evidence compelling?

7. Has your opinion on scripture changed since reading this book? If so, how?

8. Did the book change how you feel about transgender people?

9. Do you agree with the author that the direction to "love thy neighbour" should triumph over all other scriptures?

10. How do you think we can best accomplish more inclusiveness within our church communities?

11. What are your hopes or fears for the future of Christianity?

12. What beliefs or doubts do you have that will impact your ability to respect and honour the transgender people whose paths cross yours?

13. After reading *What Does God Think?* would you consider yourself more ally or foe towards the transgender community? Has that changed from how you felt before picking up this book?

14. What are your final thoughts on this writing? Do you think this is a book you will recommend to others?

Author Bio

Cheryl B. Evans was born and raised in Ontario, Canada. She is a reader and writer of non-fiction books, a lover of flavoured coffee and all things chocolate. Cheryl has been happily married to her husband, Jim, for almost twenty-five years. Together, they have raised two wonderful children: a cisgender daughter, Mariah, and a transgender son named Jordan. Cheryl is a Christian and a transgender advocate who believes strongly in protecting the human rights of transgender persons and helping to educate others.

Other books written by this author include:

I Promised Not to Tell: Raising a transgender child
In her award winning book, *I Promised Not to Tell, Raising a transgender child,* Evans wrote about her family's deeply personal journey to discovering the son she never knew she had. This non-fiction parenting memoir provides readers with an up-close and personal perspective on the entire transgender journey, from birth through age eighteen. It shares every step in her son, Jordan's, transition from female to male, and how each member of the family was affected. Although the book never began as a story that was intended be shared, it was ultimately published to help support, encourage and educate others on the topic of gender dysphoria. Here are just a few of the reviews that readers have shared after reading *I Promised Not to Tell:*

"It is very easy to read high profile books that have huge marketing campaigns, written by big name authors, but it is books like 'I Promised Not to Tell' that shape the people we become and the views we have towards others. I strongly recommend others to read this book."

"An absolute gem. An amazing book! It allows the reader to fully experience the shock, fears, joy, and triumphs that a fully involved parent of a transgender child may have. I have read dozens of books about the LGBTQ community in connection with my work on the LGBTQ section of the religioustolerance.org web site. But this is the first time that I have been motivated to temporarily suspend my work on the site in order to read a book cover to cover. Not to be missed."

"This is a must-read for every person who has a trans child or teen in their life. Explanations are clear and thoughtful. This gem of a book gives the reader insight into the lives of trans kids, trans teens, and their families in a way that will let you think, learn and support anybody on the wide spectrum of gender. The best book I have found so far."

Evans has also published a unique journal series that includes the following books:

Wonderfully and Purposely Made: I Am Enough
This is a one-of-a-kind interactive journal for transgender youth and youthful adults. Thoughtful writing prompts, interactive activities, positive quotes

and colorable images help transgender people tell their own gender story in a unique and creative way. This book makes a wonderful gift! And, it comes with three different cover options. Here are a couple reviews readers shared on *Wonderfully and Purposely Made*:

"My son received this wonderful journal as a gift. He was so excited. I read through the pages and the prompts are sure to help. I believe a person who keeps a journal learns how to deal with issues by reflections. This would be a great gift for anyone whose journey involves such uniqueness. Giving this as a gift will surely show that special someone that you love them, support them and trust them to make the very special decisions they may need to, to be happy in life."

"I think this journal is a wonderful tool for transgender preteens to young adults to be able to write down and reflect on their transition experiences. I love the quotes and affirmations and all the positivity in there. The questions are great prompts for self knowledge and introspection. I like the open style of being able to journal as the mood strikes, rather than being held to a routine. I also really like the lists that help you to organize your thoughts. There are spiritual quotes in this journal, but without it being very religious, so I think it will appeal to people of various beliefs, too. I would

definitely give this journal as a gift to a young person who is on the journey of transitioning"

My Parenting Journey with a Transgender Child: A Journal

Evans wrote this journal for parents of transgender kids. This writing prompt journal takes parents on a guided tour of their unique parenting experience. The journal will help parents of trans kids to process, explore, and express in their own words, what having a transgender child means to them. Colorable images and activities help enhance the therapeutic value of this one-of-a-kind parenting journal. When purchased along with *Wonderfully and Purposely Made* both parent and child can experience the joys of journaling together. The following is one therapist's review of *My Parenting Journey with a Transgender Child*:

"As a therapist who does gender care work with children and families, I am glad to see this new resource that helps support the health and well-being of parents raising a transgender child. Journaling is a wonderful self-care tool and this guided book can help parents uncover important insights and inspirations. Loving a transgender child is a

thing of beauty and it is my hope that this book helps that beauty shine through for families. Thank you, Cheryl, for using the love for your child as an impetus to help others."

– – – – – – – –

My Parenting Journey with an LGBTQ+ Child: A Journal

Similar to the book mentioned above this journal expands its reach beyond parents of transgender children and young adults to include parents of all LGBQ+ kids.

– – – – – – – –

If you would like to get to know Cheryl better or hear about what she has been up to these days, you can follow her on twitter @writtenbymom.
You can also connect with her through her website at
www.writtenbymom.ca

Resources

Transgender Support & Resources
Center of Excellence for Transgender health:
www.transhealth.ucsf.edu

Trans Family: www.transfamily.org

Mermaids: www.mermaidsuk.org.uk

National Center for Transgender equality:
www.transequality.org

GLAAD: www.glaad.org/transgender

Human Rights Campaign (HRC) U.S.A: www.hrc.org

A List of Churches Affirming LGBT: https://
en.wikipedia.org/wiki/List_of_Christian_
denominations_affirming_LGBT

Church Sermons
Faith United Church Sermon - An affirming message:
http://faithunited.ca/170122-a-firm-faith/

La Sierra University Church - Make It Pink! Make It
Blue! - A sermon on sex & gender:
https://vimeo.com/207974719

Bible Study & Recommended Books by Other Authors
Brian Bowen Ministries: http://eunuchflow.blogspot.
ca/

The Transgender Child: A Handbook for Families and Professionals by Stephanie A. Brill & Rachel Pepper

The Transgender Teen: A Handbook for Parents and Professionals Supporting Transgender and Non-Binary Teens by Stephanie A. Brill and Lisa Kenney

The Great Spiritual Migration – How The World's Largest Religion Is Seeking A Better Way To Be Christian by Brian McLaren

To experience the transgender journey in a very real and moving way, please check out our family's deeply personal journey in the book I Promised Not to Tell: Raising a transgender child today. I promise you, it offers so much more than you can ever learn from a textbook.

Glossary

Cisgender is a term used to describe an individual who has a gender identity that matches the sex they were assigned at birth and is comfortable (both in mind and body) living in that gender. The term cisgender is used to describe a non-transgender person. Most of the population falls under this category.

Eunuch is a noun and was a word used in the Bible to describe a person, usually a male, who were unable to reproduce. Commonly recognized as a castrated male. In the Bible, eunuchs would act as servants, usually to female royalty in the bedrooms. Female eunuchs, while not specifically mentioned in the Bible, would be women unable to reproduce.

Gender is the state of being where a person is either feminine, masculine or somewhere in between. This comes from a place of self-awareness and does not necessarily align with one's biological sex.

Gender Dysphoria is the term used to describe a person whose gender identity does not line up with the gender they were assigned at birth. This is usually the actual medical diagnosis for a transgender person and must be given before a doctor will start an individual on Hormone Therapy. Untreated, a person with gender dysphoria could feel displaced or out of sync because of the sheer conflict between their physical and mental realities. This stress can lead to depression or even suicide.

Gender Expression is a term used to describe the way one outwardly expresses their gender. Their voice, mannerisms, dress, and behaviour are all ways through which one can express their gender.

Gender Identity is a term used to describe an individual's own sense of their gender. It is the gender one feels or believes in their mind they are. This is not visible to others, as it refers to how one internalizes their own gender.

Gender Reassignment Surgery (GRS), also known as **Sex Reassignment Surgery** (SRS), refers to the surgical procedures an individual may choose to undergo to change the body they have to better reflect their gender identity. The most common surgeries are often referred to as top and/or bottom surgeries. Top surgery can be breast augmentation or removal and bottom surgery could be any surgery that alters the person's genitals. There are many different surgery types and options for a transgender person. It is important to note that not everyone may need or want surgery as part of their overall transition. Some people prefer to say gender-affirming surgery to gender reassignment surgery or sex reassignment surgery, noting that using the word affirming is as a more accurate representation to how they feel about these procedures.

Hormone Replacement Therapy is a term used to refer to the hormones an individual is taking that are not naturally produced by their body. This therapy is usually monitored by the doctor who is prescribing the hormones. In the example of a FTM, they would be taking testosterone (also referred to as "T"), and in the example of a MTF, they would be taking estrogen. These hormone medications are often administered through injections, oral medication, or external creams. All the available options should be explored with a doctor prior to deciding on a treatment path. Most doctors want to see that a person has lived a gender role experience for a minimum of one year before starting hormone treatment. The term Hormone Replacement Therapy is sometimes shortened to HRT or HT (Hormone Therapy) for short.

Intersex is a term used for a person born with a sexual anatomy and/or chromosome makeup that does not seem to match typical definitions for what male or female are. An intersex person may have a combination of characteristics that could make determining sex at birth difficult. One example of an intersex person is someone born with both male and female reproductive organs.

LGBT is an acronym for Lesbian, Gay, Bi-Sexual, & Transgender. This term is also seen lengthened to LGBTQ, with the Q representing Questioning or Queer. This term is also sometimes seen with an 'I' which, when present, would represent Intersex.

Sex is one's state of being male, female, or somewhere in between, based on their reproductive organs and chromosome makeup. The majority of the population falls into one of the two main sex categories: male and female.

Sexual Orientation is a term used to describe an individual's sexual or romantic attraction to others. A person's attraction may be to members of the same or different sex. For example, someone attracted only to persons of the opposite sex are heterosexual. Someone attracted to persons of the same sex usually identify as lesbian or gay and would be described as homosexuals. Persons who are attracted to both sexes are referred to as bisexual. In the case of a transgender man being only attracted to women, his sexual orientation would be considered heterosexual.

Transgender is the term used for a person who identifies themselves with a gender that is different from the gender of the body they were born into. The term transgender, because it encompasses so many different types of gender identity, is often referred to as an umbrella term. Simply put, someone is transgender when they perceive their gender in their mind differently from the gender suggested by their biological sex. This term is sometimes shortened to "Trans," although some transgender people find this shortened term offensive.

Transgenderism is the noun used to describe the state or condition of the gender identity conflict of a transgender person.

Transgender Man is an individual who identifies as a male, even though they were assigned female at birth. This term is sometimes shortened to FTM, which stands for Female to Male.

Transgender Woman is an individual who identifies as a female, even though they were assigned male at birth. This term is sometimes shortened to MTF, which stands for Male to Female.

Transition is a term used to describe the time when an individual begins living in the gender with which they identify, rather than continuing to live in the gender they were assigned at birth. When someone enters transition, their name and their gender expression are often the first changes they will make. A transition is complete when the individual decides it is complete. Medical intervention such as hormone medications and surgery may or may not be part of one's transition.

References

While not a complete list, the following references were used during the writing of this book.

The New International Version (NIV) of the Bible

The English Standard Version (ESV) of the Bible

Guillamon, Antonia, Junque Carme and Gomez-Gil, Eather "A Review of the Status of Brain Structure Research in Transexualism" US National Library of Medicine National Institutes of Health

ScientificAmerican.com/article/is-there-something-unique-about-the-transgender-brain/

Harvard University - http://sitn.hms.harvard.edu/flash/2016/gender-lines-science-transgender-identity/

Medscape.com article Evidence Supporting the Biologic Nature of Gender Identity

Netherlands Institute for Brain Research

Journal of Psychiatric Research

Rettner, Rachel "DNA: Definition, Structure & Discovery" LiveScience.com

Alzheimer's Foundation

Epilepsy Foundation

National Geographic

The Diagnostic and Statistical Manual of Mental Disorders (DSM)

Wise, Noel "Judge: Gender Laws Are at Odds With Science" Time Magazine

American Civil Liberties Union: April 10, 2017 Article: This Court Decision in the Gavin Grimm Case Will Bring Tears to Your Eyes.

Printed in Great Britain
by Amazon